MY JOURNEY IN KNOWING GOD!

Jeremiah 29:11"

'For I know the thoughts that I think towards you,' saith the Lord, 'Thoughts of peace, and not of evil, to give you an expected end.' "

With revelation comes understanding, wisdom, spiritual insight, and knowledge!

Rebecca L Porreco

Contents

Dedication

I am writing this book for those out there who have a call from God on their life. While others ignore the gift, or rely on their flesh to determine their destiny, know that the Holy Spirit will bring you to the place where He will introduce you. So, as you and God walk together on this amazing journey, it is to bring clarity for you to know, and others to see, while benefiting from this knowledge you have.

It is God who calls you, and God who anoints!

To my Lord and Savior, Jesus Christ: who helped me understand my life in order to write this book for others to read and learn from. "Many are called, but few are chosen." Matthew 20:16

To the Holy Ghost: who is my Master Teacher in all this! John 14:26

To my mother, Angela Virginia Porreco: who always knew I was a special child, and would call me her angel many times throughout my life, with an understanding she knew who I was all along. My mother took me to a movie at the local movie house when I was about eight years old. I remember the movie, but really did not understand the connection for revelation until recently, when I reflected upon the title while pondering. It was called "Born Free", and I am!

To my beautiful daughter, Bianca Lynn Porreco: the joy of my life, who has truly exceeded all I could have hoped or dreamed for her. When my daughter was about nineteen years old, and living on her own, I went to visit her. As I sat on the couch, just talking, I watched her work on the computer. She was multitasking at a rate that was mesmerizing to view. It was at that moment I heard the Holy Spirit whisper to me: "She is highly intelligent." This has truly come to pass.

My book is not a novel, it is an accurate account of things that happened to me in my life, as I took the Journey in Knowing God.

Listen, as you will hear what you need to hear—and it will change your life!

Foreword

A prophetic Word, given to me by the Lord on March 16, 2016 at 10:25am to 10:39am:

When He began to speak, I wrote.

"Write, my daughter, and sing praises and teach my people to worship me in Spirit and in Truth. For those that submit to Me now will never lack anything in the days to come," saith the Lord of Hosts.

"Bring your tithes and offerings to the storehouse, and see I will pour out a blessing there is not room enough to contain. You cry out for many things, and I will give them all to you in due season. That season is now," saith the Lord. "Be at peace with those who hurt you, for they hurt you without the knowledge you were My Chosen, for I had not made it known to them at the time.

"Do not quench the Spirit, for He is sent to help you when you cry. You make my heart bleed as you have bled, but those days are over and new beginnings do I decree unto you this day," saith the Lord. "And you will fulfill all your hearts desires in the coming days. It is not up to you how I do it, or even when I do it, just know that it will be done. God is with you to protect you all the days of your life, and there are many still ahead. As you grow in grace, so will your years be unto you. For I know the times and the seasons of your life, and it is well," saith the Lord.

"He honors you with your requests, and you will know those who are for you and not against you as in times past, for the burden has been removed, and the yoke destroyed because of the anointing. You have served Me well, even when others did not know the things you have done for Me. Consider the sheep of My pasture, for many do things in ignorance, but you are their teacher. You will prophesy to them for My names sake," saith the Lord.

"Trust and believe your life is changing every day, and the course you are on is of Me," saith the Lord.

"The kindness and the love you have for Me are being restored without interference. My truth is in you, and will remain and become increasingly great for you to mentor those I send you. It is written: what you stand on, and it will not be altered to please man. For when it comes to speaking My Word to those who must know what I am, saying will be spoken from the mouths of My prophets. You are one of them and will be heard in the days ahead. Be not in a hurry to fulfill, for those times will be necessary to get My people's attention: to know I AM coming. Trust My timing, Rebecca and be at peace, for the King of Kings' and the Lord of Lords' honors you today. The validation is coming, and you will know that it is from Me—and not a counterfeiter—who confirms you, and it shall surely come to pass."

Amazing, how God speaks!

God knows exactly how to get your attention. When He does you, will never forget those encounters, because they are a part of your walk with Him.

Jesus called me by my name, at age twenty-three, by my given name of Rebecca, because prior to that I was simply known as Becky. I really didn't like being called Becky, I just accepted it. For the first time since birth I knew I had a new name. However, my Father in Heaven knew my real name all along: the beautiful name of Rebecca. This was quite a revelation: to know my given name and know this is the name God knew me by. It's probably why I responded with a "what?" when I first heard Him calling me on that eventful morning, because I did not know my real name.

I asked my dad once who named me, and he said, "It was your mother who named you all." We all had been blessed with God-given names.

This is my story, titled: "My Journey in Knowing God."

Don't Judge my Journey,

Learn from It!

CHAPTER ONE

Hearing His Voice, but not yet knowing!

I was twenty years old, and eight and a half months pregnant, when I heard my name being called as if it were coming from far away.

I was awakened to my name being called: "Rebecca, Rebecca, Rebecca," like an echo, one right after the other. I quickly responded with a "WHAT!", as I was in a deep sleep—not just in the natural, but also in the spirit. This woke me up, so I got out of bed. I looked outside, only to see it was still dark, thinking it to be around 3:00 a.m.

I would usually meet my sister each morning for coffee before she would leave to go to work. We would meet out on the balcony of our adjoining apartments, have a cup of coffee together, and then she would leave. I wasn't working at the time, expecting a baby at any time. It was difficult for me, because I had a husband, even though he did not act like one. He did not stay with me most nights, because he had a girlfriend who was more important than being married with a baby on the way. He did not know how important I was to God: just treated me the way he'd learned from his own father about how to treat women.

My husband was an abuser!

This is what he knew, and this is how he treated me, until God stepped in and quickly ended the marriage. Then I began this journey to become His own.

I was so immature in life, yet somehow, I knew things maybe I wasn't supposed to know—but just did. I told my sister about my name being called, and she dismissed it as a dream. But I just knew otherwise for the moment. Something had happened, and I'd heard a voice I was unfamiliar with. Then I completely forgot all about my first encounter with God. He who loved me: who was just beginning to introduce Himself into my life.

As the Lord put it many years later, it was then He began to call me out of darkness into His marvelous light. When you do not know the Lord, you will not recognize His voice at first: just like the story of Samuel and Eli, as God spoke to Samuel as a child the first time in *I Samuel 3:4-10*. This is an amazing example of how the Lord knows His own, but we do not know these things until He is ready to introduce Himself to us. God is just God; He is Spirit!

I was so conditioned as a Catholic, going to mass. We went to church once a week and genuflected at the entrance, dipping my hand in the bowl of what we considered holy water, and making the sign of the cross. It meant we'd just blessed ourselves in preparation to hear mass by the selected priest of the week. Then we would find a pew to sit in, genuflect again, and move to the center so our big family would all fit. We'd down the knee pad, kneel down, and begin to repeat the only prayers we knew to say: Our Father, *Matthew 6:9-13*, and the Holy Mary prayers.

The Hail Mary prayer was in observance of Mary: the mother of Jesus. As the mass began, there would be the sound of an old organ being played. It sounded like attending a funeral, rather than a church service. I'm sure the songs we sang were meant to be heartfelt. However, I always felt condemnation from this music, instead of songs that would uplift my soul and take me to a place where I would want to praise the Lord, rather than just sing boring songs about Him. It was just a camouflage to keep people from knowing the real truth about our spiritual reborn nature to know our God, Jesus Christ. It is like we were kept in the dark from those who are in the dark, as if it is the blind leading the blind, until one of us is awakened in the Spirit to begin our own personal journey in knowing God.

We also had the time before mass began to go to the back of church and take a seat in solitude in the confessional booth, where we'd wait for the priest to open the little door only to say: "What sins have you committed this week?" Then we'd be absolved from our sins by repeating the traditional five Our Fathers and five Hail Mary prayers, or a complete rosary to feel like God said, "Okay, you are good for now with no repentance."

At that time, it was what we knew to do—so we did it. Just being alive, but not yet awakened.

Then the priest would come out and do many things, like making the sign of the cross a dozen times and genuflecting before the table in front of the church. It was supposed to mean different things each time it was done. But, quite frankly, I never really understood what all of it meant or why it was being done. This was the way I lived my life as a Catholic, always thinking they were holy men because they made the vow before God (as we were taught to believe).

I just went along with the program, because it was what we did in those days. No one ever thought to talk about Jesus or engage the Bible in any of our conversations, except at the dinner table to say grace. I am sure somewhere else people were experiencing the move of the Holy Spirit, but it was not my time to know these things yet. I was in a hidden place. The gifts and calling were inside me, yet to be discovered many years later.

I attended a Catholic school for eleven years, then begged my father to allow me to go to a public school. He finally relented in releasing me to go after realizing he would not have to spend the $400 tuition for the upcoming year. I hated going to a Catholic school, and wearing those ugly uniforms. I wanted to be free!

Well, I was granted immunity, and started a public school my senior year. I attended summer school after graduation because I was five credit hours short to graduate. I had failed one class during the school year, and at the end it was too late to make up those credit hours necessary. However, they did allow me to go through the ceremony with the others graduating at the same time. It was a large school, called North High School, with over 600 graduates. So, even the last year of high school I had managed to miss what was necessary to graduate, but was given an opportunity to make it right.

I did make up the time and receive my diploma, even though it came in the mail at the end of summer–right before our family was going on a vacation to California, which was the condition for me to go with them. I was to make up those five credit hours of class and get my diploma before we left.

I am giving all this information to show many of you what it was like growing up in a home that only prayed together as a family at our evening meal to bless the food on the table. This is all I knew about Jesus for the first twenty some years, until I decided to move out and be on my own. After that, I only attended church on Easter and Christmas to appease my parents. I did not attend a Christian church until I was thirty-nine years old, and what an eye opener it was! I was completely in a fog about spirituality then, but was so desiring of what it meant to be a Christian.

In case of curiosity, those nineteen years in between was spent raising my daughter with the help of my family, because I left my abusive husband when our daughter was about eight months old. When it came time to divorce my then husband, the courts decided I would be the better parent to raise my child without him, so I was granted full custody. The emotional and physical abuse I suffered while married to my daughter's father was just too much for me; I just couldn't take it anymore. Then one day, I happened to call my dad and said to him, "Dad, I need a job." He suggested I go to the phone company because they were hiring. So, I went, passed the entry test and was hired, not knowing God was with me on this next step of starting over.

There were fifty people who took the test for employment, but only two passed the first time. We were told they needed more people for a special project, and we were given another chance to take the test again. This time, however, I prayed a little prayer and asked God to help me pass the test because I desperately needed a job. I needed a way out of this sham of a marriage, and God provided that way out.

My husband and I only stayed married for about eighteen months altogether. When my daughter was about eight months old, after a few more beatings from him, I got the job and went to work. This was such a relief. I had passed the test on the second try and was delighted to know I would be able to support myself and my daughter. I did not have to take any more abuse from my husband and, honestly, I never looked back again. I began to walk forward in my life, not knowing what was next—just focusing on being a good mother and taking care of my daughter.

I remember, the night before I had to start my new job, my daughter slept an entire night without waking up. It was as if an angel in her room lulled her to sleep because I needed to get a full night's rest to be ready for my first day at my new job. I was delighted to know I could make it on my own.

After about three weeks working, on this particular morning, my then husband attacked me on one of his binge frenzies coming down from a drug high. He began to choke me, and as I laid on the floor with his hands around my neck, I felt paralyzed to do anything. We had company staying with us, but no one stepped forward to help me. Everyone was afraid of him and would not dare interfere with the beating. Finally, he got off me, and through tears I decided to go to work anyway.

As I sat at my desk with my head down, trying to work, a blonde woman from the other side of our office approached me and asked if my husband was beating me. She happened to be an abuse counselor and saw the signs. I know now God was helping me to make the decision to get out of a very unhealthy relationship. I told her "yes", and she jumped into action because she just happened to be a victim's advocate for domestic violence outside of working in this new office we were both hired for.

She immediately advised me she would come over and help me get moved out before anything more serious happened. My husband was on drugs and doing the same thing he'd seen his father do to his mother as he grew up. It was a generational cycle that had repeated itself, but God had different plans for me. I just knew I needed to try and make a go of my life without a feeling of failure to overwhelm me into thinking it was my fault. I have become a counselor as I minister to others who have had similar experiences with abuse, some many times worse than mine, to help them overcome and move forward. It is a long process because in abuse, it is the Spirit, the emotions, the heart, and the mind that are affected: not just a physical beating.

The woman told me she was going to bring her truck over and get me moved out of the situation that very weekend. I just knew I had to get away from this man, because the abuse was getting more and more severe. I told the woman counselor on Thursday to come Saturday morning; I would be ready.

She helped me move out from there to my sister's home with her husband and their son, who was only three months younger than my daughter. So, I moved out that weekend with the thought I would not have to stay with them very long. It may be uncomfortable for a time until God takes you to the next step. It's amazing how He puts an inner strength in you to move forward each day. I am grateful my sister had the additional bedroom in her place to provide shelter for me and my daughter until we could get our own apartment. As I worked consistently to have the money necessary to move, it came quicker than I thought. We just had to move for privacy, and for necessity, to understand the convenience of my move.

Right before God delivered me out of this situation, I remember being in front of the last apartment I shared with my then husband, trying to get some money before I started working. I was selling a few items like a yard sale and after a woman had stopped to buy a few things, I just said out loud, "Well, Lord, if I have to raise her myself, then so be it!" He indeed allowed that to happen. It was eighteen years of being alone, wanting a husband, and never getting to meet anyone who would fit this purpose in my life.

All because I said, "So be it!"

You must be careful what you say to the Lord because He hears. I did not realize the implication of what I had just said, nor did I really know how it would come to pass. I just knew I wanted my daughter to grow up healthy, and we would do much better by ourselves. This was my focus for the next eighteen years. Then, after moving in with my sister and her husband, my daughter and I only stayed three months before we were able to secure our own place. I found an apartment just minutes from where my mother and father lived, so it was an easy commute to work while my mother babysat my daughter.

I am telling you: God saw to it I was well taken care of and gave me support from strangers I never encountered again. I did not even know it was Him guiding me as He was helping me.

Your journey will always be different from everyone else's, and I was just living life as I knew how, but God had greater plans for me. Events occurred as I was raising my daughter that did not make sense at the time, and I was still not aware God's holy angels were watching over us. I did not see them, nor was I praying every day. Every once in a while, I would see something or someone that would trigger a "thank you" to God for my health and my job, but not to pray as I do now. God knew how long it would take to give me the necessary insight, as I drew closer to my day of knowing why I was called.

I was on my way, and did not even know where I was going. Life is full of opportunities. It still becomes a choice to walk into purpose along with destiny, whether you know all the details around you or not. I just had to trust the voice that was guiding me, although I did not know who was doing the talking. "Be still and know that I am God," He would later tell me. I was already walking towards this place called Destiny!

II Peter 3:8: "But, beloved, be not ignorant of this one thing, that one day is with the Lord as a thousand years, and a thousand years as one day."

CHAPTER TWO

On the very day I would have received my first paycheck from my new job, it just so happened my mother was unable to watch my daughter. So, I had to rely on her father to watch her. Right after I came back from lunch, I got a call from my soon to be ex-husband and he advised me I was to give him $100 at the end of the day, or else he would not give my daughter back to me. Yes, he did that to me, even bringing her by on my break as if to taunt me, so I would give him the money he asked for. He wanted to be this man about town, with a charisma he gave the acquaintances he was associated with, with the idea that he was in charge—or so he thought.

I was just happy to see that my little girl was fine, so I gave him the money and kept right on moving forward. I kept thinking: *Why did I make such an awful choice for a husband, and then a father to my daughter?* Actually, she was the only blessing from this union. God always gives you a good thing out of a bad situation; it's all how you look at it. So, no matter what happens in life, look for the rainbow.

I like to call the Hand of God in it, because it shows up after the storm.

It was amazing I was not hurt more, because many of the women he was with after me ended up in the hospital. Their beatings were far worse. After I moved out, he had no more control over me, so I was making good decisions for both my daughter and myself. He really didn't seem to care too much that he had responsibility now and had crushed my heart in so many ways. It just took eight times of being hit, slapped, and humiliated by this man—some worse than others for me to realize. It just was not what God had planned for me. At the time, my ex-husband did not know that soon he was going to permanently be taken out of my life.

When God makes your life line up with His purpose, you just move in it.

One of the last times he hit me was a morning I will not forget!

He came home mid-morning after a night of partying, and decided it was my fault things were not working out. We argued in the bedroom, and he began to punch me in my face and then in my abdomen. I felt the blow and it was so hard, I urinated on myself. I could not help it, it just came out. I kept screaming to him, "Don't hurt me, I have to take care of the baby!"

She was only three months old at the time, and all this commotion made her upset, so she began to cry. Apparently, my sister was home at the time and without me realizing it, he had left the door open. My sister came rushing in and told my husband to stop and to leave me alone. She had to push him away, and then he just stormed out the door. I called the police to report the incident and had to give a report of what happened. I was so embarrassed my whole body was hurting and my nightgown was wet. I described what had happened the best I could.

I felt such remorse for ever allowing this person into my life in the first place and asked: *How could I have been so naïve?*

God uses everything for His good to accomplish what He desires for us. Even though this sounds like a horrible experience (and it was), it also taught me to realize how much more God loved me. He provided a way of escape to begin a new life.

I did not grow up in an environment like that, so when he would hit me it was foreign to me. I would see my mother and father argue, but my father never hit my mother. I am sure if I would have stayed with him, it would have been the same thing over and over again, year after year. So, God helped me to decide to end this marriage and put my life back together without me even realizing He was my future, not this man. God was beginning to take control of my life, even though I did not have an idea who He was just yet. He shows you the way where you should walk, and you walk it.

The scriptures I found in *Isaiah 45:4-5* helped me realize the Holy Spirit was already doing things for me before I could even give Him any glory. While trying to recover from this last episode of spousal abuse, there was a knock at my door. When you are hit as hard as I had been, it takes a lot just to get your bearings and gather yourself together enough to live each day, one at a time.

My landlady happened to come to my door to see if I was all right. In our conversation, she said, "I'm going to retire, and the owner is looking for someone to take over managing the apartments." God was already moving on my behalf. I thought about it for a minute and told her I was interested in the position. In a few days, I went for an interview. By then, I had forgiven my husband. He came with me to the interview, and we told her we would be able to run the building for her. He would do the maintenance, and I would rent the apartments. Another opportunity for just another mistake to allow this man to stay in my life.

Would I ever learn?

This only worked for six months, and by then I was sure to get away from him for good. Sometimes it takes a while to get your freedom, even though God is with you. He is walking you into something better. Somehow, I just keep walking with a strength that came from the One I was just beginning to know.

It was almost a year later when I asked my then husband for a divorce, because I knew the marriage was not going to work. When I told my husband I was going to divorce him, his reply was, "Do you know how many women would give anything to be in your place?"

I answered him with, "What are their phone numbers?"

I was getting a boldness about myself that was not there before. I would have called each one of them personally to tell them do not get involved with him. He was an abuser. It stemmed from a generational curse. His father also abused his mother during their marriage, so it was just being repeated. Of course, he was not like that in the beginning. He was charming, and I fell for this charade. It's like something happens to trigger the abuse and, in their eyes, the wife is always to blame for what happens. The Enemy masqueraded himself, and instead of waiting for God to bring a husband suitable for me, I fell for the counterfeit. The Counterfeiter always comes first! That is a revelation for many.

My father is the one who came to my rescue, who paid the lawyer $500 to dissolve this marriage under irreconcilable differences. I was too young to be married and all this was just an avenue for The Enemy to try and take me out, but it did not work. The Lord set my feet upon a rock, and He was ordering my steps now. He was giving me lead way to make my own decisions, because I did not know it was Him behind the scenes, watching my every move. Nearly eighteen years later, I began to understand.

My lawyer introduced what I didn't want to believe at first was infidelity. Of course, the spousal abuse was also introduced, for the sole purpose of having full custodial rights of my daughter. Infidelity, commonly known as "having an affair", meant something thirty-nine years ago. Now, people won't even bother to get married.

My ex-husband did not come to the divorce proceedings, so I was given full custody of our daughter. I was truly on my own and still did not fully understand who was helping me along the way. I did not stop to give God credit for any of this, but I did feel a relief after almost three years of always being a victim. I didn't pray much, but I knew my heart was screaming for help. So, God rescued me because of His love and His plans for me. I tried one last time after the divorce to get back with my daughter's father, only because he told me he needed a place to live. He was such a trickster and a liar, and I always felt sorry for him. He was just using me again, so he could make the current woman in his life suffer a little—trying to salvage another disaster waiting to happen.

Well, the truth was, he had broken up with his current girlfriend at the time. He was just using me to get back at her, and had no intentions of staying. I will say this to get it off my chest: during this time, we got into an argument in the kitchen. My little three-year-old came out and told her father, "Don't you hurt my mommy." He decided to push her backwards and she fell. He said, "Now go to your room," and we continued to argue. After we argued, he just left. But that night, as he was sleeping on the couch and I was so exhausted from the emotional trauma from earlier in the day, I picked up a knife from the kitchen.

I walked into the living room because I was really going to stab him in the chest. I wanted him to die for all the hurt and pain he had caused me. When I was about fifteen feet from him, I heard this voice saying, "It's not worth it." In that God moment, I put the knife back and went to my bedroom. I cried as I went back to sleep, just wanting him to get out of our apartment.

The next morning, he announced he was leaving to go back to live with his girlfriend. If I would have known to say "Hallelujah" at that time, I would have. It was so bittersweet, because I was working to provide a home for our daughter. He just wasn't meant to be in the picture, and yet my heart had yet another thorn thrust in it. So, for the next fifteen years this was my life: going to and from work, raising my child, and showing her stability so she could grow up as normally as possible, without ever seeing physical abuse from her father towards me again.

Years later, about fifteen to be exact, after I had finally forgiven him, he came to me and apologized for all he had done. He told me he did not realize what he had until he lost it. In the moment, I believed he really meant what he said. Although we stayed divorced and he would skirt in and out of her life, I was the one who supported us through the job God had provided for me years earlier. He did not want to pay child support, and avoided the system completely by quitting his jobs each time Social Services would contact his place of work to garnish his wages. I would estimate that, over eighteen years, he gave me less than $3,000 in child support to help me pay for our daughter's care. He was trying to hurt me more, by thinking it was just more money for me to spend rather than to provide for his daughter.

Divorced, and deciding for myself I would raise my daughter the best way I could, I depended on my parents for many things. This included child care and the general necessities that helped get all my needs met and errands done. Even though I was working full-time, there never seemed to be enough money at the end of each paycheck for a car. I normally would have about seventy-five dollars left over after rent was paid, so I would have my dad and mom take me and my daughter shopping at Kmart. This was our treat every other payday. I bought new outfits for my daughter and would squeeze in something for myself, along with what necessities were needed until the next pay period came. So, for the time being it was what I did: call my dad every time I needed something or had to go somewhere. It was just what I did, not knowing there was so much more ahead for me.

This seemed to work out fine for a while, but I truly wanted my independence. My dad was doing so much for us, it was like I never left home because we were always together. I would leave my daughter with my parents in the morning, and take the bus to work each day. This was a benefit for all, because it kept my mother busy throughout the day, and this kept her out of the hospital. You see, my mother had a mental illness all during my upbringing and into my adulthood. I did not understand what or why this was happening to her, but we all dealt with it the best we could.

The doctors were always putting my mother on all kinds of medication. Hard drugs were prescribed, such as Thorazine or Lithium to name a few, and so many others were slowly killing her. The doctors would also give her electronic shock treatments each time, and it destroyed her ability to think for herself. None of us knew what to do to help her, but seemingly as she watched my daughter during the day, it was like therapy for her. She had a responsibility, and it was keeping her from losing her mind.

I remember one time, my mother took herself to the hospital during a weekend, and I needed a babysitter for the upcoming Monday. My dad was still working then and could not take time from work to help with this situation. I was desperate, so I contacted an organization known for helping people and they referred someone to me. I thought she must be all right because of the referral.

I went to this woman (I do not remember her name) who happened to live literally just two blocks around the corner from my parent's home. I would drop off my daughter each day, thinking she was in good hands. After two weeks on a Sunday morning, my daughter, being only two at the time, was standing in the middle of the living room area. She just stood there for a moment, then opened her little legs and began to urinate on the carpet. This action immediately alarmed me, knowing my daughter would never have acted in this way: it meant something was very wrong.

I told my father, "She is trying to tell us something, and we better listen to figure out what was happening to her." It was so unlike her. She was always so responsive to my mom and my family. Always loving and laughing with a sweet demeanor, so I immediately realized it was out of the ordinary.

My daughter was completely potty-trained, so I asked her what it was. I told my family she was just trying to tell me in her own way this woman was mistreating her in my absence. I had trusted this woman with my child, would take her there each morning with this facade of love she displayed. There was nothing more than a demon inside that woman, and as soon as the door shut she would lock my child up in a hall closet to torment her throughout the day. I was shaken by this event, and I handled it the best way I knew how. She would smile and wave at me as I left, and then put my baby in a closet while I was gone. Only this action from my daughter brought it to our attention. How alarming it was!

It is so important to pay attention to your child's behavior, because they try to tell you when something is not right. But God was there, and He knew what was going on! You can only imagine the horror I felt after finding out what kind of a monster I was leaving my daughter with during those two weeks. I did not have spiritual eyes to see with then, but His Spirit was watching over my daughter.

You see, my baby, even though only two was potty-trained, able to eat on her own. She was trying to tell me that as she was being shifted from our loving home into an entirely foreign environment. I gave charge to this woman, who was doing her harm in my absence that was more than I could bear at that time. I would leave my daughter in her care, and by her actions, she made my daughter act in a way to expose the demon. Of course, at the time, nothing in my life made me aware about demons or spirits because I wasn't spiritually awakened yet. My daughter didn't know how else to express what was happening to her. I had allowed this person to watch my child, not realizing what was going on behind closed doors. But it finally came out and when it did, I went off. Just so you know what this means, I spoke my mind, I let this woman have it verbally. My desire to be as protective as possible caused my mothering instincts to roar like a lion, and to find out what the hell was going on. My spirit was angry!

This was God's way of showing me that something was wrong: through her relieving herself on the floor. When I went there to confront the woman, she shut the door in my face and would not talk to me. I alerted the organization who had referred this woman to me immediately about the incident, and I suspected there would be an investigation. However, I did not push the matter any further. It was like I knew God would take care of that woman in some way for doing this evil to my daughter. Even though it happened to my child, it would not happen to another.

God will take of our enemies, He just does.

I was so upset and angry. I just called my mother, and told her how desperately I needed her help to watch her granddaughter. This worked because it brought my mother home. It was as if something clicked inside my mother's mind, and she came home from the hospital on her own without even realizing what had happened in the past two weeks. It was a plan that worked: my mother took over as if she was never gone and our lives were back to normal again.

I only know all these occurrences happened to bring me to an awareness of spirits in people being used by The Adversary (Satan) to set up a sting against me and my daughter. But, before you are made aware of this, you only ponder about it. I did not know to pray and ask God what to do, because I did not understand how to ask the question yet. I did not ask until my daughter was eighteen, and by then I wanted to know what was going on. Why had all these terrible occurrences happened in our life without explanation? Yet, somehow, we always came out all right. I had a need to know, and I wanted an answer to my "whys?" Far too many things had already happened to us up until that point, but I knew answers were coming. I just did not know how I would find out, and from whom I would get my answers.

Even though it took some eighteen years for me to respond to God completely, it was the perfect time for me to come to God and ask that very important question: "Is this all there is to life?" It was what brought me to seek Him: to find out more.

"His ways are not our ways, and His thoughts are higher than our thoughts.": *Isaiah 55:8.*

God knows how long it will take for you to truly answer Him. This was only the beginning of my journey, or so I thought. Many things happen along the way in life, but as you come to know your Father in Heaven, He reveals the moments in time that are hurtful to you, because you have a desire in your heart to understand. My need to know was stirring all along, and by the time I went to the altar to give my heart to God, it was the appointed time He had planned for me. I wanted Him to protect me from any further disappointments. I needed to ask for His help. I just didn't know how.

Once later on, after another attack from The Enemy almost took me out, I had this very large rosary I hung on my bedroom wall. I was so shaken because I did not understand spiritual warfare at all. I took that rosary down off the wall, laid it on my bed, and crawled in the middle of it. This was my way of telling God I wanted Him to protect me from whatever it was that caused me to feel unsafe. I did not know how to talk to God, and I did not know He had a voice to communicate with me. I was never taught this in my eleven years of Catholic school in a class called Catechism, which meant a class on religion. Not once was the Holy Spirit mentioned in the pages of that book. We were forced to read just nonsense, only to keep us in the dark. We were taught by priests and nuns, who most of the time were nothing more than demons in dark clothing. Not one of my teachers in my classrooms ever gave me the feeling of security: they were always just looming, about to disguise what was inside themselves. My mother was very discerning, and I must say the tiger would come out of her at times, when any of her children were threatened.

One time, my mother almost pulled one of the nun's habits (head dress) off her head because I would come home crying about how badly I was treated in the classroom. It was in second grade at this same school. My mom came to school with me, and they had a little discussion in the back of the room. I know my mother had a few words with this nun because she came back into the room a bit disheveled.

Just thought I would interject that here. We were taught priests and nuns were respected and regarded because they were supposed to have given their lives to God. What a false statement that is! Only God knows what goes on behind closed doors, and even though we were taught to respect them, my mother was much wiser when it came to the care of her children. When my mother passed on in 1998, I had to look through her things to clean out what was in my mother and father's bedroom. My sister and I discovered pictures of Jesus and prayers in her dresser drawer, next to the closet. I was so moved by this, it brought me to tears. Why? Because just forty-five days prior, I knew my mother had accepted Jesus Christ as her Lord and Savior. I knew she was in Heaven; it was a knowing inside me.

CHAPTER THREE

As my daughter and I were getting used to being on our own, I was at my father's house on one of our regular Sunday get-togethers. They included dinner and sometimes a family trip to Walmart.

For some reason, we were all discussing something and then I said, "Where is my daughter?" because she was usually always in someone's sight. I went out through the front door, and walked across the front lawn and the paved driveway to the neighbor's lawn. I got there just in time. I saw my beautiful daughter about to be attacked by a huge dog. I reacted, I believe, like most mothers and grabbed my baby before that dog could do any damage. It is amazing to sense something is wrong and just begin to move. It was an experience I will never forget. My feet carried me swiftly to where she was about to get attacked.

Of course, it frightened all of us and my daughter began to cry as I held her in my arms to comfort her. I thought: *I will never let her out of my sight again.* The neighbor came out. I questioned him about why this dog was not tied up, and told him what could have happened to my little girl had I not come out when I did. Honestly, the holy angels of God were truly watching my little one, and somehow my eyes began to see.

Even when you do not know He is with you and your child, or husband, or family, He is there to bring comfort, peace, protection, and love. So, as the day approaches for Him to reveal Himself, try to understand that The Enemy is always trying to destroy you before you discover who you are. God is always in our midst, even though I had no idea that He had great plans for me and for my daughter, just yet. Sometimes it just takes us longer to get to the point for us to realize we know it's Him always working on our behalf, to keep us out of harm's way, and what He does to keep us safe. Angels all around!

My family was supportive in many ways, and I depended on them to help me raise my daughter. Of course, we had our squabbles and we did not always see eye to eye. But, always, my family and I would make the best out of our different personalities. We would fight and then we would love to the same degree—many times in hidden ways, only to discover a new side about each other.

My mother was my babysitter, and my dad was our transportation. My father, retired by then, would be there to pick up his grandchild from school and help her with homework because I was working. So, as my life went forward, God was providing for my daughter and me through my family, but I did not realize all the provision He was giving me until many years later. God is gracious and very patient as He waits for us to recognize the goodness is from Him. He just blends those around us in His sovereign effort to help us through each situation, even though we do not know who really to be thankful to until the time of revelation for everything. I had a Bible: a nice, pretty, white one with a beautiful picture of Jesus on the front. It was mostly for decoration though, because when I tried to read the words, it was hard to understand what I was reading. I wasn't born again yet!

I was growing up along with my daughter, together as some would say, because I did not remarry and that was why I said earlier: *Be careful what you say.*

It was a family tradition to meet every Sunday while my father and mother would fix dinner. We would sit at the table with this huge crucifix in the dining area and there Jesus was, hanging on the cross. We had no real knowledge of a resurrected Savior at all. We would pray for the meals before we began to eat, but that was it. No other time did we discuss the Bible, or even attempt to talk about Jesus in our home as we grew up. We just didn't; we only knew to be thankful, and that was life for a good portion of my growing up.

You could say, this was the Lord keeping me hidden until it was time, and everyone has a time to know God. Whether you accept Him or not, everyone will have an encounter with Jesus, even if you deny Him. I mean to really know and understand Him. It doesn't happen all at once, but surely as we can handle it, He will reveal many things that will take place—and even what we will be doing in our lives. I honestly did not think about God too often in the next eighteen years as I was busy raising my daughter, unless I was in trouble. The only question I would keep asking God was: *why does this keep happening to me?*

It was the same thing over and over again. I would meet people, male or female (in other words I would let them in my life so easily), and completely trust them. I did not understand why I would make such foolish decisions: because I was so vulnerable. And yet, He was watching over me. Not realizing then, my worldly attitude about life kept me in that place of always needing to be rescued by a God who I had yet to truly encounter. He was my deliverer each time, without me even knowing I needed to be delivered. He was my helper, even though I wasn't asking for His help until after I was devastated by the current hurt. I am sure everyone understands. It just seemed to happen to me, much too often. He is a friend who sticks closer than a brother. Each time I found myself in yet another mess, He needed to get me out of it. The door of escape would open, and I would go through it, still not yet knowing it was God who was making the way possible. I am so hoping this will help someone as they look into their life, when things are hopeless and they do not know which way to turn: the Lord, our God, makes a way.

So, I would first call my family, tell them of my woes, ask for their intervention of assistance, and not put the two together. He would use them to help me each time. You see, when you are the chosen one in the family, and you do not have a clue what that means, your siblings and parents will wonder many times: "What is wrong with you?." Neither you or they have an answer. Even then still, I would force myself to go to church on Christmas or Easter, because this is what I was supposed to do for my faith in Jesus—to be as real as I could possibly make it. I just didn't know what faith really meant. It never really dawned on me to cry out to God, but as a Catholic that was all I knew to do, because I had yet to be introduced to the One who was watching over me. I honestly would go just as a duty, not to make myself feel good, or to be free from something. It was all I knew to do. It was a walk only, no prayer, no life-giving words being taught or spoken, no one to pray with me or even for me. At least that is what I thought. It is the Spirit in the Word that brings forth the Revelation of His Word to you, His child.

Even as I would pray the recommended five Our Fathers and five Hail Mary prayers or the whole rosary from the confessional at the back of the church, it was only what I was taught to do. So, I did that believing God was giving me yet another chance to get it right, after each trip to see the priest where I'd confess my sins.

Never once did I hear pray to Jesus: I was always told pray to Mary, Saint Joseph, or some other patron saint to help with whatever I needed at that moment. Each one had a purpose for me, or so we were taught. This would sometimes make me feel better, but the moment would pass. Then I was all alone again with no idea what to do next.

Somehow this kept me for the time being, which ended up being most of my life: until age thirty-nine. A lot can happen to you in thirty-nine years, but when I heard about

Jesus, that is when things began to change in my life. It was not much of a comfort to see my Savior on a cross, not knowing He was there because of my sins, but also for the sins of the world. I would try hard not to look at the fixture of the cross with Jesus just hanging there, still bleeding, because I did not understand completely why He was on there or why we even needed a statue to remind us of anything. What I needed to know: He is risen; that is the difference.

I honestly never thought much differently after each mass I would attend. I just had an unusual feeling that what I was doing wasn't sufficient, and yet I could not explain it. I believed the rituals of a church service should somehow make it better, but they didn't. I needed to know Jesus. He was drawing me toward Him, little by little and step by step. The Lord patiently waits for each one of us, but when you realize how long it takes some of us, especially when we have a call of God on our lives, we go through things to bring us closer to Him. He will speak to your spirit to help you know when it's time to come into the Kingdom through salvation. This is only the beginning.

It is to know the One who walks before us and with us at the same time. I found out later, this was a journey to find out who God really is, and not appear to be close to God because I had just confessed my sins to a priest the last time I attended a mass. I would hear that opening statement: "And what sins have you committed this week?"

I would confess the same thing as usual, as I was taught to say since the last time, trying to think hard about how many did sins did I sin, or really which one had I sinned, or what was the most current sin to be absolved from? The priest doesn't have the credentials to wash away your sins, nothing but the blood of Jesus will do it. He did not die for your sins; Jesus did this for each of us.

I came to find out, it's not the priest who has the power to forgive sins: it's the blood of the Lamb, Jesus Christ, who forgives us each time we fall short. It says in *I John 1:9*: "If we confess our sins, he is faithful and just to forgive us our sins, and to cleanse us from all unrighteousness."

But, when you do not know the truth, you do what you know to do—or what you were taught to do. There were many other instances that happened to me that didn't make any sense throughout the next eighteen or so years, but I honestly did not ever think to lower my head and just ask God what this meant—or what to do about it. My survival instincts were in control, not my heart. However, He would hear my hearts cry, and always respond to show me a way out. He was leading me to Him through burdens, trials, mistakes, and tribulations.

It was amazing how God allowed all this to happen, while seemingly waiting for me.

And wait He did, to the tune of almost eighteen years, before I decided for myself there was something more I needed out of life—and it was Jesus.

Time after time, as I was trying to just live life, the spiritual attacks sent to destroy me were unexplained. They were sent to stop me from knowing who I was, because there was something God invested in me that I did not yet know. You see, when a call to something is unfamiliar, it is very hard to explain what you are feeling: you just know it's something.

The spirit realm wasn't made known to me until many years later. I sometimes would see or hear things, but they would frighten me into not saying anything or talking to anyone about it, until God brought me to a place where I had to know who He is. I was getting closer to know what all this was, going on around me.

The demons aren't afraid of you until you let them know you aren't afraid of them. When you show fear, they can sense this and will take advantage of you every time. But, when you know the Word: *Luke 10:19*: "Behold, I give unto you power to tread on serpents and scorpions, and over all the power of The Enemy; and nothing shall by any means harm you," it will keep you somewhat of a hostage until you find yourself asking the One who created you to reveal the truth: His Word. This is an amazing transformation of your mind and your soul, coming to know who our Creator is and just how powerful He is. Yet no one really talks about Him.

I did all the things of life the world's way and just wanted to enjoy my life because that is what everyone else was doing. I would work through the week and then come Friday night. My friends and I would use that term lightly. We'd call each other, meet at the current hip spot to party, find a man, then have breakfast—only to find ourselves in the same scenario every other week: just a different playmate.

Yes, I slept with many of those playmates. I decided for myself this was the way to find love, because that was what the world was showing me. Through television and conversations, all real nonsense because the spiritual side had not been made known to me. I was asleep spiritually and my time to be born again, awakened to the Spirit, was becoming more and more real to me. I was vulnerable to the world, until the Word revealed to me: I am in the world, but not of the world. I'm just passing through to an eternal destination.

I would sleep with these men time after time, never to hear from them again. I wanted so badly to have a real relationship with someone who cared for me and would stay in my life. After each time, things would go wrong: not hearing from them again, only to find myself alone after I gave my body to them. I was searching for love, but this was not real love. I was young and naïve about life, but I had to learn what God needed me to know, often the hard way. I made decisions as a way of escape instead of trusting God. It was a cycle that went on for many years, only to discover this was not what I really wanted or what I thought I needed. Still, searching in all the wrong places for what only God could give me. He just patiently waited and waited to introduce Himself to me. Yes, it took time, in fact years to finally ask for His help. It was in the asking that started my moving towards Him. Amazing love!

On those occasions of partying, my dad would make me leave my daughter overnight with them, so as not to disturb her sleep when deciding to come home after 2:00 a.m. on a Friday or Saturday night. You know the song: "It's Friday night and time to party." He was keeping me even in my sin.

Well, I did this for about two to three years, then I just stopped suddenly. Desiring or looking forward to those Friday nights was no longer an anticipated time anymore; it just wasn't appealing any longer. I just wanted to stay home, be a mother instead of my parents doing this job, and get to know my daughter. Thank God for my parents, who did not judge me. They were just there to help me through each obstacle, and try to give me wisdom for me to grow. They knew I was searching and were always there to help me.

During my time of promiscuity, I probably slept with twenty or more different men. I do not even remember most of their names, nor did I ever see them again. I would meet them at a club or wherever. Then, at the end of the night, I would just go with them, have sex, get up the next morning, go pick up my daughter, and go home. My spirit was so restless, as I would feel different each time this happened, without a clue what was happening to me spiritually. The world was filling me up with junk, and I needed to be delivered from it.

I did not know that each time there was a sexual encounter, I was sleeping with The Enemy, and each time my spirit was being contaminated more and more. During those years, I had two abortions and each time I ended a life, not knowing what I had really done. These were unwanted pregnancies at the time, so I just took care of it, not realizing this was not what God wanted me to do. If I conceived in lustful sex, I should have kept those babies or adopted them out, through the mistake of having sex outside of marriage. I began to ponder one day about the welfare of my children. As I did, the Holy Spirit explained to me my mother (who had passed) was raising my children and they were fine, waiting on me to reunite with them in Heaven. How merciful, and yet how gracious, our God truly is. I know what the world can give you. I thusly discovered what my Heavenly Father would offer me: eternal life, as I had never thought it would be like.

The world is so deceptive in creating ways to destroy lives that could have grown up to be deliverers. God will use every mistake we make to show us just how amazingly He thinks of every minor detail in our lives to give us hope and refuge, and to help us to overcome the worst of what we have done to ourselves. His love far outreaches anything or anyone—no matter what! Mercy and grace are the greatest gifts God offers us every day. When I read the Word now, I go directly to *Psalms 103:1-5* to know the daily benefits.

I made horrible mistakes, not realizing the impact or the result of what I had done, but God has forgiven me. Yes, I repented for many things I did as I was living life the world's way. The Lord told me to include this in my book, because I know He wants to use this as a testament to His unconditional love, grace, and mercy as this will reach others wherever they are. Know God wants to heal them from the sin of abortion. He is the redeemer, deliverer, healer, and restorer of my soul, and this He can and will do for them also. Jesus died for us to be saved, even when we do not know we need a savior.

After I accepted Jesus Christ as my Lord and my Savior, He began the process of cleansing what I had polluted. I went through seven years of cleansing, and then another seven years of purification, to rid my temple of those worldly encounters where I did not realize what it was doing to me. The Holy Spirit was giving me allowances, and then pulling me back from certain harm, only to protect me along the way. I just did not know it yet. There were no sexual encounters during those years, just total purification from what The Enemy was using to try and destroy me. Yes, it frightens me to know what was happening to my spirit during those years of meeting men and sleeping with them. It made my deliverances take much longer: to cleanse my temple of each thing that could have killed me before God could use me.

I was being prepared as I was going through, so I could minister to someone else for a later time in my life. I would move in with my parents, then move out. It was back and forth for many years because I just wanted to be on my own, yet I was not ready to be on my own. This would take some time, but each move I made caused me to become stronger, and the desire to survive was getting greater. I just did not know I had an adversary trying to kill me. My father would say to me: "Out of my four children, you are the only one who always seems to give me trouble." All I could answer was: "It keeps finding me."

Those moments of: *How could this happen to me again?* I'd end up back at my parents' home and then resent the decision once I was there. It wasn't that my parents did not love me, I think they just did the only thing they knew to do: allow me back home to learn those lessons I had to keep repeating for some reason. I was living outside of God's will for my life, because I did not know I was purposed for something far greater than I knew.

Many years later, I did ask Him and He took me through each time and place while explaining: not only did I have a call from God on my life, but my daughter was also going to be used by God in a mighty way. It takes time to absorb all the intricate details of the "whys" of life, but if you are willing, He will reveal each one to you. Each instance of destruction was to stop what God had placed inside of me, and inside of my daughter, from ever coming to pass. The Adversary to our souls was out to destroy us even before we knew anything at all about God, or His purpose for our lives.

CHAPTER FOUR

My daughter was such a beautiful little girl. I put her in dance class when she was about two and a half years old. She excelled in her classes, which consisted of dance, tap, jazz, and acrobatics. Every week she would go and dance to her hearts content. The dance company would also have a yearly dance recital with costumes for each girl: ages three to eighteen. It was so much fun, and my daughter took these classes until she was about eleven years old. When she was five years old, she entered a Cinderella Pageant, as they were called back then. She had won several titles in previous pageants, but the most memorable was when she was crowned Miss Cinderella for the City of Aurora, and we were invited to be participants for the Parade of Lights during the Christmas season that year. It was so cold that night, about six degrees. I drove a convertible car down the street, only to remember the voice of a woman that rings in my ears occasionally. She said to the person standing next to her, "Look at how beautiful that little girl is."

It's a pleasing memory I will cherish forever. These parades still happen each year in Downtown Denver. I'm telling you these moments of my story because there always seems to be danger lurking and waiting to strike, even when you are just trying to enjoy life as it presents itself.

Then, when my daughter was about six years old, I met a man through someone I worked with. We had a two year off-and-on relationship, if that is what you want to call it. He was a drug dealer, unbeknownst to me at first, but even when I found out how a dangerous he person really was, it did not frighten me off. It only made me want to make him a better person by staying with him and showing him what I thought was love.

A dream became a nightmare, and little by little I was sucked into a dangerous world. He was always in the streets, making money and rarely available, unless he wanted to show me off. If you do not understand what that means, I will try to explain. Some drug dealers do double duty as pimps and he did both. He was too busy running the crack cocaine house he owned, making money illegally. It was a dangerous avenue to be involved in. So, again, without me knowing that God was watching over me, He once again intervened, because of my worldly mindset that had not yet been corrected.

One night, I came to visit him, and I parked my car a few feet ahead of his current location. We had just come from dinner and as we were talking in the living room, when we both heard a crash coming from outdoors. After going outside, we discovered a huge branch from the tree where I was parked had fallen on the back of the car, shattering the window completely. When we returned inside, this man said to me: "Do you think God is trying to tell us something?"

The hair on the back of my neck stood up. It wasn't too much longer after that the day when I realized it was over. God was making a move for me, and He was making changes in my life to get me to a different place before The Enemy could take my life. I know God was in control and intervened at this specific time when I came home early from work one day, only to discover as I was pulling up towards the garage area where I lived, a U-Haul truck leaving. I thought to myself: *I wonder who is moving out.* I went upstairs, only to find out it was the drug dealer I had moved in with. He'd stolen mostly everything, including some of my things, leaving the townhome we lived in almost empty. He was not expecting me to come home early that day. It was just in time for me to discover I was dealing with the Devil again.

I was so angry and upset about this situation, as I soon discovered my boyfriend had no good intentions for me at all. He was a killer and was doing what he wanted because I was in the way. I was alarmed at the trickery of someone wanting out of a relationship to pull something as low as this.

But it had to happen, and God was right there to protect me from further danger.

When you read *Psalm 103:4*, He is saying to us: "I will redeem your life from destructions, and then I will crown you with loving kindness and tender mercies." It was time to end that situation, and it ended by removing me from certain harm, because I did not know how dangerous it was becoming. This is exactly what the Lord kept doing for me my entire life, without me realizing how many times I had done this—only to be rescued again and again. This is how badly I wanted someone to love me, and yet it was only God who would give me the love I was so desperately in need of.

I told this man he was a coward, and as he came toward me, he lifted his fist above my head. It came down on the top of my head so hard, my knees buckled under me and I collapsed. The force of the blow was just too much for my body to handle, so down I went. I recovered myself and the last thing I said to him was: "I'm calling the police to press for assault charges."

I did make the call, and the police took a report over the phone. It took a few weeks for them to arrest him, but I am telling you, I could feel the anger from this exposed demon who would have destroyed me had it not been for the hand of God. When God delivers you out of a snare, it happens in ways that do not seem even real. He was constantly watching over me during all the disastrous mistakes I kept making.

After he was arrested, we did go to court. He was fined $200 for the assault charge, with no further jail time. While we were in the courtroom, I was being cross-examined by his lawyer, and he asked me the question: "Was I romantically involved with this person?"

Before I realized it, the response that came out was: "No!"

I just blurted it out, because prior I had been falsely accused by the drug dealer's current liaison of all kinds of lies while she was on the stand. Everyone in the court just stood still, because after this was blurted out the whole demeanor of the court room changed. His lawyer had nothing to go on, so no further questions or any more interrogation could continue. All because God was again in control, and keeping me from going down with this person.

I was so hurt emotionally through all of this, and yet another thorn had been thrust into my heart. I had asked a friend of mine to come to the courthouse with me for support, and she could not believe it herself. The attorney this man had hired was out to cut my juggler vein in the process of trying to tear me up one side and down the other. I was questioned and questioned about things that brought us to this courtroom. When I responded with a solid "no" concerning my relationship, the whole situation changed. It closed their case against me, which was to try and destroy my reputation. It did not work. I did get my belongings back, because his lawyer made him do the right thing. The following week, here my dad was again with his truck: to retrieve my furniture that has been stolen the month before.

After it was over, people came up to me and said they had never heard of anything like that happening before. I couldn't even believe it myself. When I left, I looked at him and just shook my head, never to see him again.

I could have been killed from the blow to my head, but God kept me and already had begun to heal the trauma of this disaster. I found out later that this same man, who tried to destroy me, went to prison for about ten years, not to long after we were separated. I never heard from him again.

This is the reason all of this had to happen, because the Lord was preventing me from getting caught along with the drug dealer and going down with him. This would have destroyed my daughter and myself, I have no doubt of that. But God made sure I would come out a winner! You see, whoever you are connected to, The Enemy wants to destroy also, because they are the next generation. So, if he can get to you, the next one in your lineage is your children.

Understand this well, so you can discern what has happened to you was only to stop what God put in your belly. Every generation has an appointed Joseph!

My mother and father came to my rescue again, allowing my daughter and me to move back home for a brief amount of time, to help get me back on my feet. The Enemy was trying to destroy me in every way possible, even before I could even identify who I was spiritually. But God is always triumphant when you are one of His chosen, even when you do not know it. I am giving someone my life story as they think back on how many times He had to rescue them from things they had no business getting involved in.

It is always a trap, but God always has a way out. I love this scripture in *Romans 8:28*: "All things work together for good, to those who love God, and are called according to His purpose."

It takes time for all things to be made well again, and He rescued me again from yet another plight I had caused. What I'm trying to say is the deliverance comes, but it takes many years after to heal from the trauma of abuse your spirit may suffer in the travesties of your unwise decisions. It doesn't just effect you physically, it is also emotional and spiritual abuse you need to heal from. This takes a complete and wholeness in being delivered, and it may take years to heal completely!

When I hear preachers say: "just get over it", this to me is not what needs to be said. It needs to be ministered properly, because it does take time to heal spiritually, emotionally, and physically for the heart to become whole again. No matter what happens to you in life before you know the Lord, He will walk you into wholeness, so you can know Him. I am a walking wonder as I write this book, because even as I look back, it is hard to believe all the things that happened to me—yet I survived.

<u>God is with you every moment of your life, even when you do not know Him yet!</u>

Earlier in my life, my father wanted to discipline me many times, and my mother would always step in front of him to protect me from him laying hands on me, if you know what I mean. She would say "Now, Ralph," and he would always step back.

Of course, I realized what I was being blamed for was my fault at times. However, some of my punishments were severe, with a rod of discipline that was too harsh. It did hurt my spirit. These are wounds in my heart that still effect me, sometimes even to this day. So, the result: I began to hate any authority, especially from men. This made it hard for me to submit when I started to attend church, because

I was spiritually aware of what my father did to me. I will explain it this way, so there is no error in misunderstanding what I'm trying to say here.

When I was about seven, maybe eight years old, a little friend of mine from up the street came to spend the night. The night before I had found a tiny brown mouse and wanted to keep it. So, I found a wooden crate, got a screen from the garage to put over the top, and positioned the box on the side of our house. It was about seven a.m. the next morning and my father, with his booming voice, woke us up and called me into the kitchen. He asked me a few questions about what I had done and before I knew it, my bottom was exposed, and the beating on my behind was a much more severe punishment than I deserved.

What my father did not know was the punishment did not fit the crime. His version of a spanking was so damaging to me, it stayed with me for many years to come. I went back to my bed, and whimpered for about an hour before I got back up, because at that time my father had to go to another job and was gone. It put a thorn in my heart because in my little mind, I could not understand why my father was so angry about me wanting to keep a brown mouse and protect it. However, God did.

I do not know how God dealt with my dad about this, but I am quite sure it came up. He had a plan for my life, and being abused by a father who was supposed to love and protect me was a part of the plan. I cannot fault my mother for any of this, because there were times when she knew not to interfere with the discipline any of her children received, no matter how severe it was.

The significance I am trying to imply here is that before you hit a child, calm yourself down and rationalize before you decide the punishment. Not only can you cause emotional trauma, but the spiritual hurt incurred can bring more harm than you think. When you have a child who has a gift, it is so important to realize early on how precious they are to God first. I know my father did not know how much it had hurt me, but it started a growing hatred in my heart for him, and it continued to grow into a rebellion against men throughout my adolescence and into adulthood. Even now it is very hard to submit, although I will to the Lord because He is far gentler to me when I know I must go further with Him.

I would not respect my father as I should have, and although I grew up with him being the father figure in our home, I hated him for the many spankings I received as a child. This is just an example for those who are reading my book, to understand the damage we can do to one another if we use our authority upon someone in the wrong way for whom we are responsible for. I know everyone is different, but this is how it effected me. I healed from many wounds that were forced in my upbringing. The day I received revelation of just how much I was wounded and had been carrying this pain around with me for so long was the day I realized just how much God really loved me, despite what people did to me or what they thought of me. He is all I have, and He is my Redeemer and the lover of my soul!

Someone needs to know this today: the pains of yesterday can shape tomorrow—if you allow the Lord to minister His grace and His love to you today.

CHAPTER FIVE

The next time I heard this voice in my ear, it warned me as I was walking up the stairs to my apartment, thinking about a trip I was planning to the Bahamas.

Yes, to meet with yet another man I had become acquainted with at a happy hour after work one Friday evening. I heard this voice saying: "Don't go!" as I was climbing the wooden stairs to my apartment. My daughter and I lived on the upper floor of an older home, and the staircase was old. It would squeak at our door entrance. Of course, I thought: "Whose voice am I hearing?", and I just decided to ignore it.

I went on my trip anyway, not having any idea it was an angel assigned to my life. It was a warning about this trip, and the angel was giving me an instruction. He was in charge, and I needed to do what he said—or at least take it under advisement.

Well, I didn't listen, and went with the intention of having a good time, trying to start a new relationship. I decided to go because I had never been to an island before. Being a single mother, I was working hard. I was thinking about how deserving I was of this trip.

It was a disaster, and I mean a disaster. He just left me to fend for myself, even to the point where my hotel bill would not be paid. However, my trip was salvaged, somewhat, when I met his family on the second night I was there. His sister, Mia, came to my aide. She became the person who took me out, and showed me a great time for the duration of my mini-vacation. Long story short, I did not learn my lesson about men. I wanted love each time, only to find I had made yet another mistake in picking the daring, wrong ones.

God had a plan for my life, but it was not yet time for this to begin. Because the time had not yet come to fully know, I was being allowed to fall—only to get picked back up by taking these risks in life. Each time, I was striving within myself to gain some strength to move forward after each failure.

This was an eighteen-year battle of ongoing mistakes, only to recover what dignity I had left, and keep going. If anyone can say I was meant to be a great one, without going through all the things that brought me to write this book, I truly would have said you are kidding. "Me? Why would God choose me?" But, He did!

Somehow, God just kept preserving me because of the gift inside me, keeping my daughter from knowing too much along the way. She was such a precious little girl, and I can honestly thank God for her not being touched by any of this. He had His own plans for my little one, who was growing up so fast right before my eyes: even to the point of having me encounter yet another angel on another stairwell that said: "If you do not change the way you are raising her, you will destroy her."

By the way, if you think God doesn't hear the cries of your own children, He does and He will respond. This got my attention quickly, and I did a 180 turnaround. I was doing all the right things for provision: like a home, food, and clothing, but the love she needed and desired was not being given. I fed her, bathed her, and kissed her—but it wasn't enough.

I needed to give her all of me, and the love I was desperately trying to find for myself, she also needed from me. God kept coming to me in different ways to show me how to take care of myself and my daughter. I absolutely, from that day forward, began to do more for my daughter than I had ever done before. I paid more attention to her, in fact, putting her in front of my own needs. I was beginning to listen.

I do not understand why it takes some of us longer to come to Christ. I am just giving my readers my story, and I know everyone's is different. They just are. These are all true encounters that occurred in my life to help me find the One who loved me the most. Even as I began to go to church, I did not find the love I thought would be there.

<u>One of my deliverances:</u>

Once again, I found myself dealing with a man in my life and desiring to have a relationship with him, only to realize he was not ready to settle down and had probably several other women at the same time as myself. I always had the thought: *This one would be different*, being drawn by the wrong kind of love. It is the love of God, not the fleshly love, you give to someone that makes the union complete.

It's amazing to me how men are just not the way they were when my mother married my father. They just do not make them like that anymore—or at least that is what I thought. I was not aware of the spiritual preparation for a man or a woman when God's hand is on them. It's called equality. The man is to be the stronger one in the union, yet never to lord over his spouse: but to build her instead.

I was looking for a man to understand me, not for the pleasure my body could give him, but to treat me like a queen, as my father did my mother. The unfaithful men are always searching, but not looking to God to build them both. It's a mistake many have made. Quite often, they mistreat the one woman in their life who should be a priority when it comes to maintaining the relationship. Too many times, men involve more than one person in the space where there should be only two. It then becomes crowded, and someone always ends up getting hurt.

The wounds we suffer through our relationships can only be the snare in which The Adversary wants to destroy us, because we are not basing our decisions on God's will for us and through His Word, which give us guidelines to follow for each day. *Amos 3:3*, says: "How can two walk together, except they be agreed?" It's a question we must ask no matter what the relationship is between a husband and wife. We must always be vigilant of his devices, as revealed to us in *I Peter 5:8.*

One day, I just got fed up and said these words: "I will not sleep with another man until the Lord brings me my husband," not knowing how those words would bring forth my deliverances as I spoke them.

About one month later, after I had broken up with this person, I was laying in my bed, tossing and turning with restlessness. I decided to go into the living room to lay on the couch, thinking this would help me sleep. I laid there for just minutes. Suddenly, while I was in a half-asleep, half-awake stage, my mouth dropped open. I could feel a dark figure leave my body. I asked: *God, what was that?* I did not get a response, I just drifted back to sleep. The explanation came many years later, when it was brought back to my attention. It was then I inquired: "Why?"

I had to come to the knowledge of spiritual matters to find the spiritual answers.

These deliverances come as only God can orchestrate them, because they are spiritual deliverances. Most of the time, they do not happen at the front of a church. They are personal and take personal care from the Holy Spirit to ensure a complete deliverance. God is sovereign and very concerned about His daughters and sons aligning with Him, and experiencing what he has in store for us. He watches over us with the swiftness of a hawk, yet with the watchful eye of an eagle. He's ready to rescue us, coming to our aide at any given moment to deliver us from any impending dangerous situations.

Well, many years later, pondering this moment, I asked the Lord to show me what I'd experienced. He explained it to me as <u>I spoke the Words of my own deliverance</u>. He had sent an angel to me, who commanded the evil spirit in me to leave—and it did.

The angel told that perverted sexual spirit: "You heard her, now come out!" It left me that very moment.

When man attempts to deliver you, it is only temporary. When God delivers you, it is permanent. I was on my way to being made whole.

I pray someone, when reading this book, will be healed by understanding things are often our own fault, but God is in control. He will keep us until He prepares us for our deliverances. We do not realize when we allow The Enemy in, because he is so subtle in his devices. Yet God will bring us out. When we cry to God for help, it begins to set things in motion. So, you see, you do not always need someone at church to lay hands on you, nor do you need to be in church for God to deliver you. When you speak your own deliverance, it will happen. It is the perfect timing, each time! Angels are dispatched to us, but they must travel through the Second Heaven to reach us for the answer to prayer, or the resolution to a circumstance. Even though The Enemy tries to stop them, they will get through. So, my angel was sent for my own personal deliverance, because I said it with my own mouth. The request was heard, which put this in motion.

One of the men I had previously slept with opened a door for this ungodly spirit to enter me during our sexual encounter in the first place. Yes, this would seem to be privileged information about my personal life. Yet, if it will help someone somewhere understand that spirits transfer—I will speak out about it. I was not born again for the Spirit of God to be in me at the time. When you ask the Holy Spirit, He will reveal understanding to you. When He is calling you and you are not yet responding, trying to figure things out on your own, listen to Him.

I not only wanted to know, I needed to know. As I was delivered, I took another step in the direction of God. He brought me to a place of complete surrender, so I could walk with him. I needed to walk through what I had allowed the world to do to me. I needed to come out, so I could bring others out of the darkness.

There comes a time when you turn from your wicked ways, and discover the loving God who was there all along, waiting on you to respond. Yes, He is my Deliverer!

The Lord let me know it was my own decision to become spiritually clean from all those men (twenty—and those were just the ones I remember!) I had slept with over the years, trying to find love the World's way, but God revealed Himself to me with another plan for my life. I began to know my Heavenly Father in ways I'd never thought possible.

Many years later, I asked the Lord why it took so long. He said He had allotted time for me to raise my daughter before He would call me again. I was busy doing my own thing, while He was busy preparing me for my deliverances. Yes, there were a few more to come when it was time for them to manifest in my life. It was when I responded to the invitation to salvation my understanding began. We think we know what we are doing in life, but it takes the One who created us to show us the way to go—and how to get there. All else will fail. As you look back, you will see the truth in it. For every mistake we make, there is an ultimate solution. God never allows those chosen to get beyond His reach.

A huge interruption!

Now, fast forward two years.

I was about thirty-five years old. The company I worked for told us they were downsizing, and to put in transfers in other locations so I could keep employment. I did. Soon, I was picked up by an office in Seattle, Washington, and moved to Bellevue (which was across the bridge from Seattle). Just the two of us—my daughter was fifteen at the time. She was so angry with me when I told her we were moving there, and I tried to convince her it would be a new start for us.

My daughter, of course, did not buy it! Taking her away from her friends and having her go to a new school was just not what she wanted. It was not working, but she had to come reluctantly, anyway. It's being away from family that gives you a perspective about life, and how much we really need each other. I wanted to get away, and see if life in another location would be better than where I was at the time. It was a new start for us, and to a certain degree we were better there. I realized I had a lot to learn again about life.

My mom and dad, who always came there to visit us, made us feel connected to our roots. I really discovered what true parenting was during those seven months we were gone, and began to understand just how much my parents had helped me raise my daughter.

I found I was more miserable, away from what I knew, and so was my daughter. It got to the point where one day a supervisor came to me, and said, "Rebecca, you do not look happy here at all. Did you know that you can still put in transfers to go back to Denver?"

I was elated to hear those words, and began the process of putting in the paperwork immediately to get the ball rolling. However, right before she came over to me, I remember bowing my head at my desk and saying to God for the first time: "If there is any door you can open to help us get back home, would you please open that door?"

And behold, my supervisor walked up to me within five minutes, and spoke. He was waiting for me to ask for the help only He could give. If you think for one second that God is not aware of your concerns then think again, because He is. He was drawing me back to where I needed to be, and I was willing to cooperate this time.

Did I fall on my knees and thank Him?

No, I did not, but He was waiting for that day to come. God is so patient with us, even when we do not know to thank Him on the spot. My thankfulness was coming in a much bigger, broader way. God is aware of our entire lives.

About one week into the process, I was picked up by a department back to Denver. The transfer went through, and we were on our way home within two weeks of making my request known. The amazing thing about it was right after my transfer went through, I was told the door for transferring within the company was now closed. Had I not put in my paperwork at that exact time, I would have been stuck for two more years in Seattle until the freeze was lifted and employees could transfer again. This was truly a God Moment for me.

Of course, I did not attribute any of this to God. I was just delighted to know I could go home again. But something in me was beginning to resonate that this Jesus, who I really knew nothing about, was more a part of my life than I'd realized.

This was my first real encounter with God moving on my behalf, which brought an awareness of His existence to me, as I finally asked Him for help. I have no doubt He had done more without making it known until it was time for me to know. I would cry, and He would respond without me realizing it was Him moving and arranging things around me each time. God hears a whimper and God hears a cry. He responds to us because that love between us is developing every day as He shows us how much He cares.

A little later, I became aware—not only did He hear everything I said, He had a voice and this voice was who I was hearing all along. He was quite able to speak to me. This, of course, was after I gave my life to Him through salvation. I began to understand it was Him leading and guiding me all along.

I told my daughter when the transfer went through, because I did not want to say anything until I knew for sure. We both celebrated with such delight because she was just as miserable up there as I was. Wrong decisions became apparent, yet the best of results can come about as God turned our lives back to where we should be. The time was drawing closer for me to step into His Kingdom and to live His way for His purpose.

While still there for a few weeks, I went to a farm on the outskirts of Seattle to buy my daughter a kitten, just to help with the loneliness she was feeling. She had to leave her school and friends to go with me, even though I thought it was a good move to start over. We found ourselves right back where we needed to be. Please know, I loved God in my own special way, yet each time He stepped in to help me was the only time I even thought about Him. I still did not understand I could have a daily relationship with the One who created me with a great purpose in mind. I was not taught to know all the things I needed to know about the Lord.

I was learning as I went, mistakes and all.

God will wait for us, no matter how long it takes. It just takes some longer than others, so do not give up on those you see. They do not look like much, because He is always working to get us where we need to be, and become who we are called to be. *Philippians 1:6* says: "Being confident of this very thing, that He that hath begun a good work in us, will perform it until the day of Jesus Christ."

Just a Note!

Oh, yes, The Adversary meant to destroy me and my daughter many times throughout our lives—even to this day. Even when I was still in my mother's womb she developed toxemia, which could have killed both of us. God knows from the moment you are sent from Heaven, being fashioned to become His, that The Enemy wants to kill, steal, and destroy what God placed in you. It's the gift, it's the call, and it's the anointing he does not want to come to pass. The Enemy was kicked out, and he hates God and everyone from God. He wants to destroy us.

I lived what I thought was life, not knowing there was so much more going on around me. I needed to know who God is—to help me see what I could not see. I failed each time I tried to fix myself in this world, thinking it would get better than the last disastrous moment. Yet I just kept moving forward, because I had the holy angels of God assisting me. *Psalm 91:11-12* and the Holy Spirit were guiding me.

I remember my father asking me, "What are you doing to cause these things to happen to you?"

It appears I was always in trouble, my life turning this way and that. I didn't know it was a spiritual adversary after my soul, so I would never discover who I really was supposed to become.

A part of me wanted to stay in that place of despair over the last tragic thing that had happened. Of course, it did not occur to me then, but as I began to search myself, I discovered just how valuable I was to God. He began to show me I was the one chosen in my family to come in first, like a Joseph.

My family dismissed all of this because they only knew me as Becky. God knew me as Rebecca, the name He gave me. My name means "Earnest Devotee" to the Lord.

I am yoked to the Lord, and cannot be moved because of purpose. God gave me the title to this book: "My Journey in Knowing God." It was not to find Him, it was to know Him. Each time we cry out, He rescues us or comes to our aid.

How powerful—to have such an awesome God watching us, even when we have yet to discover who He is. It is a revelation!

CHAPTER SIX

When we returned home, things got back to normal. But, within one year of our return, my life began to change again. In the new office where I was transferred, I met a woman named Leslie, and she began to talk to me about God. Although I am sure Leslie meant well, she was giving me too much spiritual information for me to digest. This is where the gift of discerning is so important when you disciple anyone who is a new convert. Everyone is truly different, and each one's walk with the Lord will be their own significant journey. It is imperative to know the voice of the Holy Spirit when you begin to disciple and minister to know where someone is in their personal walk. Give them exactly what they need, not too much, just the right word because you may never see them again.

She gave me books to read, and so I did. The books she gave me were too much for me to absorb, seeing as I was a new Christian. I wasn't ready to know all this information, and it was hard for me to get a proper perspective.

She told me to watch this movie: *The Green Mile*, which was far too much for me to grasp as a new child of God. I mean the movie made me not want to know and wonder, instead of helping me with my walk. I asked her not to share anymore with me, because she was not being led by the Spirit.

I will say this now: if you are a disciple to anyone, please remember to ask God first before you offer advice of any kind. God knows how and where that person is in their walk and how much to give them. It may not be the right time for you to offer them a book called *Piercing the Darkness* yet. The book opened my eyes, but it did not do me any good because my Spirit was not ready for it yet. I just did not have the heart to tell her.

So, please keep that in mind as you mentor anyone: listen to the voice of the Holy Spirit before you say anything, because He knows. We all learn at different levels, so that is why I am saying, "Hear from the instructions first before you offer anything more than what someone can understand at that time."

It was the Word of God I needed to establish, not reading nonsense from a worldly perspective and calling it spiritual. God calls us as disciples to help someone understand things they do not know, but if it is too soon for them to know, you can be more of a hindrance than a stepping stone.

I am going to introduce you to another woman. I will call her Nancy, who also worked in our office. She was divinely part of my first real blessing from the Lord: our first home.

I distinctly remember asking God for a home with a beautiful street name. He is listening as you speak the desires of your heart. She suggested this real estate agent, who was a friend of hers, to show us the market of available homes. I will call him Larry because honestly, I do not remember his name. He came to pick me and my daughter up one Saturday morning and took us around to ten different showings. It was the tenth one, and as we drove up to this townhouse, I saw the street sign. It was called South Cimarron Circle. We parked in front, and as we walked up the stairs to the front door I was delighted by the many amenities, but my mind was totally on something else. It wasn't until I walked in the kitchen, and stood at the window, that I felt this overwhelming feeling the house was mine.

I belonged there.

My thoughts were interrupted. We went downstairs to see the basement, and I was told it would be finished before I moved in as a term of agreement in the sale. It is amazing to me how many people God will use to bring you right to the blessing He intends for you to have as it comes together. Seven people were involved in this process, and they had all lined up according to His will, just for me.

God blessed me and my daughter with our first home, and it was beautiful: from the location, to the neighbors, to my commute to work—and He did it just for us. It all worked out amazingly! I gave Him thanks for this wonderful new blessing, because I knew it was the Lord putting it all together. Well, I was just delighted at the prospect of being a homeowner for the first time in my life, after paying rent for seventeen years. When I think about all the attempts I made to secure a home before, and all the money I wasted just doing what I wanted without the wisdom to secure a future: of course, I could kick myself!

Finally, I was ready to be a homeowner. I had thought many times before that day about having a home for myself and my daughter to enjoy. I did not have the $3,500 necessary for the down payment, but the agent told me I could ask my father for the money. It was called gift money, which I had no idea about, but I was learning one step at a time. This meaning, I would not have to pay it back, and this money would not be included as an outstanding loan amount on the paperwork from the bank. I went to my father immediately and asked him for the gift money and he said, "No!" so quickly I just hung up the phone.

My heart sunk, but my mother became a tiger. She went after him concerning it, because he did have the money to secure the loan application. God was working through my mother to bring about something that was meant to be mine.

The next morning my father called me, and said he would give me the money. It was like bells went off. I just knew that home was ours, and it was beautiful. We moved to our new home within thirty-five days, and both my daughter and I couldn't have been more excited. God is always detailed when He blesses you with something you have been wanting for seventeen years. Amazing!

We had our first home together, and my daughter was going to graduate high school very soon. It was a three-level townhome, the end unit, and it was less than one-year old. The couple we purchased it from just wanted a bigger place to raise a family. It was just perfect for me and my daughter. So, we moved in, and we were getting settled as the invitation came to go to church for the first time in many years. I was used to going only on Easter and Christmas. It was as if all the things God wanted me to have along with knowing Him were being done as my life came together. Imagine that: I begin to receive the blessing before I even knew what it meant to be a Christian. It was my time to walk as a true child of the King.

Finally, about one year later, I took the step to want to know more about God.

I was on my bed one morning, and I looked up at the ceiling and said this: "Lord, is this all there is to life, going to work, coming home, making dinner, and doing the same things over again?"

Well, He heard me. Within one month of me asking the divine question, here I was attending my first Christian church service, where I answered His call to be saved. I did not even know about salvation, because I already thought I was saved.

This was quite an experience: to acknowledge Jesus as my Lord and Savior, and ask Him into my life during that service. Now I knew for the first time, Jesus was no longer on the cross. He was living in my heart. Growing up as a Catholic, Jesus was always on the cross, still bleeding in any Catholic church I went to. This was all I knew until ... I spoke these words: "Lord, is this all there is to life?"

He answered me again.

The church I was invited to was close to my home, and my friends met me there, even though they attended a different church at the time. My salvation wasn't as dramatic as some can be. I just went to church, listened to the message, and when the altar call was made I raised my hand. Then I started towards the front, with soft tears running down my face, and a new warm feeling in my heart.

I remember the altar call, responding to the preached message as my hand went up, and going down towards the front of the church. I felt such a warmth inside my heart for the first time. I looked over, noticing an usher who was watching me with tears coming down my cheeks, and thinking: *He knows I just got saved without us ever saying a word.*

It was an intense moment, yet ever so sweet, feeling a new sensation I had never felt before. The pure love of God just flooded my heart for the first time, and I was swept into a new way of living. From that day on, my life changed dramatically.

When I did notice the usher and he looked at me, I could almost hear without words being spoken, him saying to himself: *This one really got saved today.* He knew! I had a realization something had just happened to me, but I did not quite understand: Jesus was now living in my heart!

Unless you have been in a church all your life that teaches the true word of God and who Jesus is, then it takes some longer to truly find out who the King of Kings and the Lord of Lords really is. He doesn't just enter your heart: He is there to protect and guide you throughout your life, for you to know you are blessed and an extension of His love for others. You are to be an example of Christlikeness. It is the drawing of this amazing love that brings us to a place of surrender—and then we truly begin to live.

I am only saying this because, as I began to remember certain things in writing this book, there were those moments He revealed so much to me when I asked Him into my heart. It wasn't too long after that I began to think hard about my life, and what had happened in it. I mean, so many awful things had transpired for those first seventeen years after my daughter was born. I wanted to know why this or that had happened.

He began to take me backwards in my life, and show me my life in the Spirit. I was upset, angry, and disappointed, all at the same time. He explained to me, although He was there watching me stumble and fall, He was always ready to pick me up. Each thing that happened to me, and why it happened, was an indication for the first time: my life had spiritual significance! I just did not understand what was going on around me. So, the Lord took me by the hand, and began to show me what it all meant.

He was so gentle in His explanation of the how, when, and who so I would understand. I know it was because many times I did not ask for His help, even though it was available, that these things happened when they did. The Enemy of my soul was truly trying to take me out before I discovered how powerful God had made me. When you don't know, you just don't know. Part of the reason I am writing this book is to tell those who don't know, like I didn't: there is more to life.

Hopefully, they will respond many years earlier than I did, so they can have this very experience of God in their lives to lead and guide them through it. It doesn't take a village; its takes being born again. *John 3:5-6* puts this into perspective.

Don't wait to find God; He just wants you to know Him. It takes time to reveal to you all the things you will need to know on this journey called Life, but be assured: God is involved in every part of it. As I began to grow more serious about what was in the Word and getting to know my Heavenly Father, He gave me insight to spiritual knowledge, understanding, and wisdom about many things. Some things I did not ask to know. He would just show me, because it was important for where He was taking me. The desire to question Him on things that had happened to me in life began a quest within myself to know what I was experiencing. I remember one day, as I was reading the Word, I came to *Jeremiah 33:3*.

When I spoke the Word out loud, it was like I went to this place in the Spirit, like I was moving without moving. I asked God: "What are all these things I don't know?"

He was showing me what He meant, so I would learn about Him. My steps were being ordered of the Lord so quickly, I could hardly catch my breath.

The Lord did all that and more. He gave me the gift to discern spirits, and the spiritual realm they operated in. It doesn't just mean seeing a spirit or spirits, or the people being used by unclean spirits, it is also to shows you how to deal with The Enemy. Many people do not even know what is going on inside them. But somewhere, somehow a spirit or spirits gained an entry point, and they came in. When you discern carefully, you can see how the person is being used, how it got there, and how to pray them through: if the timing of deliverances is now. You must pray and ask God to tell you what to do next. Everyone needs deliverance from something. Why else would we need a deliverer!

When God reveals something to you about someone you know or don't even know, you must pray first for Him to lead you in how to pray for someone and to take the next steps. A quick "God Bless You" in passing just won't do. As a true intercessor, I go before the Lord, pleading the blood of Jesus and then asking Him to create in me a clean heart and right spirit as I go into prayer for that person, situation or circumstance that only God can do something about. It's the power of the Holy Ghost that accomplishes deliverance within the person you are being led to pray for. I do not have to know, God just shows me your face and if I get a name I speak it. You could live in another country, and I can still pray the Word of faith for you to be delivered out of the very situation you find yourself in. In the spirit realm, there is no distance or time that a prayer cannot be heard and God begin to move for you.

Prayer is the essential key in a believer's life to have communication with God. It helps you to know how to pray! We should all be intercessors for ourselves, our family members, and others we may meet on a day-to-day basis.

Staying obedient to a lifestyle of prayer will strengthen you spiritually and you will hear His voice more clearly. People aren't doing this because it takes submitting yourself to the Lord to use the knowledge of His Word and the gifts properly in interceding on behalf of another. Sometimes, we are not supposed to do anything, God may be trying to teach someone something without our interference or interruption. This is the time, we ask God for wisdom.

Understand *I Corinthians 3:6*, "Some plant, some water, but God brings the increase." You must be led by the Spirit to proceed. In other words, as you disciple or minister someone, hearing God's voice is most important to know what to say or say nothing at all, just pray. Then you will know, are you planting a seed, watering a seed that has been planted already, or just sit back and observe as God brings the increase to the seed already planted. God is patience in waiting just as a farmer is in waiting for a harvest that was planted earlier. We are all called to be seed-sowers. I know I learned to be one and I must admit God was really after me to know more much sooner, I was doing all I could to hear His voice before I did anything on my own ever again. He had work for me to do. He gave me much understanding as I became a willing vessel. It is a constant submitting to the will of God for anyone to be used by God. His desire is that none would perish, but all coming to the knowledge of salvation.

One woman I was acquainted with told me years later, she had been praying for me for almost ten years, when I saw her one day and told her I was now a child of God because I received salvation through Jesus Christ: she cried! You just don't know how much prayer it takes for you to come into the Kingdom. It doesn't matter who has planted or watered those seeds in your life to bring you this far. It is good to give thanks for the ones God uses to accomplish this.

After all, it had taken Him forty-one years to get me this far. I don't even count the first twenty-two years, because I was in a hidden place as a small child until my time came. It's amazing how you can reflect on your life, then God brings clarity to your every question on what happened up until this very moment. He will show you all you need to know for all the gray areas of your life to come together and make it understandable.

When you put this into perspective, in the book of Genesis, it clearly says one day is like a thousand years to God, so He had waited a very long time for me. My encounter halfway to the altar that day was not a milestone, it was just a knowing in my knower that everything would be different from that day forward. There have been many twists and turns in this journey with God and much of it, I must admit I did not enjoy. I had left out the most important factor and that was putting God in the equation of life first. It was for me to find out that He has been watching over my life and helping me even when I did not know He was the one doing the helping.

So, as you grow in grace finding out how powerful you really are spiritually, you will have gifts revealed to you so God can use them to touch and change lives for yourself and those around you. I am called to minister, and as He has taught me along the way, it just works well when He is doing all the driving. I know when to approach someone, what to say to them, and how to say it, so it produces a birthing of revelation in them, not make them feel worse. It is called building those into whom God reveals them to be. You are just the worker He chooses to use.

The reason I say it like this is because I was discovering God in ways that had to be taught by God and God alone. I wanted Him to bless me, to keep me, to mold me, to demonstrate through me, and to cause me to walk this walk so I would come forth as pure gold. Just be willing and be prepared because you do not know the end from the beginning as He does. Yes, He gives you visions and perspective information along the way, but you also must go the way He wants you to go that has been prepared for us to walk in it.

Be prepared if you ask God for this, because I did not expect to go this route. I was an innocent babe in Christ learning to walk by faith, to hear and recognize His voice, so I could follow His instructions. No, I did not always get it right. It was a learning process, and He gave me a grace learning curve as I decided within myself to move forward. People are not so good in giving the grace and mercy that God gives you, even when they themselves have received it, but soon forget how much love it takes to minister. Just to remember without love, all your efforts are for naught. It means nothing to God. He will send another to repair the damage you caused.

Most times, you get dismissed by others before you even realize what happened, but do not let that stop you from knowing God for yourself. His grace and mercy go much further than any other could give. God is revealing Himself as you discover what it is about you that makes you special, set apart for a purpose you never considered until now. Once you know who He is, you can walk with Him. It truly makes your journey much easier. You will not become bitter, you will become better.

Even as my own family dismissed me for calling myself a Christian when I told them I did not want to attend Catholic mass any longer. I wasn't getting anything out of it, and this was caused quite a stir when our times spent together was being directed to Jesus. My father was especially harsh as he told me, "You're going to hell, for not wanting to stay a Catholic."

Can you imagine hearing this from your dad? It saddened me a great deal, so I would just leave and go home to cry on my bed alone. I wanted my family to come to the true knowledge of Jesus Christ instead of believing He was still hanging on a cross for personal observance, not a revelation.

Ralph (my father) just did not understand the plans God had for me. It takes the Holy Spirit continuously drawing you away from something to bring you into where He wants you to be. Little did I know, God was planning to do was have me minister to others who were deluded in their minds about Jesus. Through Catholicism, the Lord told me that Catholics only know the Jesus who is still on the cross, and are thinking Mary has more power than her Son, Jesus.

This is what God wants His children to know, no priest, no saint, no statue in a church will be able to save you, deliver you, set you free, or to answer prayer. You must call upon the name of Jesus to be saved, not a priest to absolve you from your weekly sin. They do not have that power or the authority. Only the blood of Jesus, who went to hell to get the keys to sin and death and overcome The Enemy for us. Now we have the power and authority to do the same, when you step into His Kingdom and acknowledge Him as Lord, then you have the promises of God through the Word.

When you look up the Word "Catholicism" it is defined as the faith, doctrine, system, and practice of the Catholic Church. Jesus is not a church or a church building, He is not a doctrine or a system, and He is no longer on the cross. Jesus is the head of the church. He is risen and this purpose for Him to die for our sins, gives us the rights as a true son or daughter of God to be born again. It gives us access to God the Father through His Son, Jesus Christ. He rent the veil in twain to unite us again, it's not just a union, it is a reunion. This is showing us, His children, who we really are as being righteous through the blood of the Lamb and the purpose of why the cross was allowed, this found in *Matthew 27:50-54*. It took me awhile to understand that no sin I committed then, and even now will keep me from my Heavenly Father because of the shed blood of Jesus. Yes, it does take repentance to maintain this awesome relationship, but it is for us to be who we are called to walk as after and to live by.

At that very moment, when Jesus gave up the ghost and He spoke: "It is finished", God reconciled Himself back to His people to have the relationship with us again through His Son, Jesus Christ, since Adam broke the covenant back in the Garden of Eden. The most powerful revelation: God Almighty had already chosen Jesus Christ before Adam sinned just as He had already thought of you coming to the knowledge of Christ before you were even conceived in your mother's womb. He is Alpha and Omega, the beginning and the end, our Redeemer.

As I was being taught to walk by faith and not by sight, I did not understand how people who say they are Christians could say and do the things they do without understanding the completeness of the death, burial, and resurrection of Jesus. This was the reason I wanted to do things for others, and bring His truth from my heart to those who have yet to know Him. I want people to see and encounter the One who is called Love. For you see, without love in what you are doing for God, as described in *I Corinthians 13:1-3*, all your efforts are nothing more than a tinkling cymbal or a sounding brass—if done without the key word of Love in it. A lack of the display of love from the heart is nothing more than a fleshly attempt to win someone to Christ, but your efforts will be fruitless. God, through His Son Jesus, is the Love needed to win those who are lost. No one will know this until you show it to them.

Before I leave my home at any time of the day, I always ask the Holy Spirit to give me the ability to show the fruits of the Spirit (which is God's character) to those I may come across, even if I'm just going to the grocery store. People need Jesus. They need to know who He is, and what He has done for all of us. It is not a club you happen to join, or a place to hang out on Sunday morning. There is a spiritual awakening going on right now, all around us. We are either going to be a part of it or not.

We are all responsible for ourselves, and those who see us every day. We must be an example, which says we are the true sons and daughters of the Highest God. I want people to know I am a child of God, and I am not ashamed of saying Jesus is Lord, knowing what He has done for my soul. You must have a boldness about yourself that says: "I am a Christian, and He is the King of Kings' and the Lord of Lords'. No one and nothing will come before Him, or between Him and I, as God gives me the strength and courage. For each day, I must do His will."

It is this knowledge that will present itself as we come out of who we were into who we are. I am no longer conformed to this world, I am transformed by the renewing of my mind. I believe what the Word of God says about me. I also want others to know; this is for them also. As a disciple and a minister of Christ Jesus, I take full responsibility for who I am, how I carry myself, and what I say to those around me, representing Jesus as an Ambassador for Christ. It is not a duty to perform, it is a burden I carry to bring souls into the Kingdom of God. For as the Lord showed me, Hell is wide open, yet Heaven is not nearly full.

Glory to God, I am excited just typing this on the page right now!

CHAPTER SEVEN

When I was invited to a Christian church for the first time, God met me there in a very gentle manner and quiet way, although He had been with me all along.

It was my first decision in finding out who God really is. I did not realize it, but there were a few times in my life where I would hear His voice and not know it was the Lord speaking to me. This may sound naive to some, however, in my upbringing as a Catholic, we were not taught to even know God speaks. God will reveal Himself to you in a way that you will know it is His voice and for you to recognize it. *John 10:27* says it very clearly: "My sheep know My voice, and I know them and they follow Me." This begins your communication with the One who spoke you into existence. Wow, just think about it for a moment.

When I went to church on Sunday mornings, with my family of five, we never heard the priest say God talks to us, yet alone speaking in tongues or praying in the Spirit, a God-given gift. So, I did not have an understanding that He was available for a conversation. I didn't know He was watching over me, waiting for me to respond. It took almost forty years to say "Yes!" to the Lord! However, even though I did not know Him, God was working on my behalf every time something awful happened in my life. I would always cry out to Him for understanding. My question was: "Why does this keep happening to me?" I didn't understand. Before I could rationalize the situation any further, God would already have an open door for me to escape, and to make me feel safe again. I did not know who God was, I just knew His Name, as most people do. It's not just the Catholics. It's the Baptists, the Protestants, the Pentecostals, the Episcopalians, and the Universalists, etc. All those who have a name of religion in their own terms, without the Revelation of Jesus. They all claim they know who God is, but they do not have His Spirit or the love of the Father through the Son. I'm sure someone can relate to this, because we became aware He is a person of a trinity called the Godhead: meaning the Father, the Son, and the Holy Ghost. Each One different, yet all in agreement, together as ONE.

I want everyone to know, I loved God from the very moment of birth, I just didn't know why. This may sound indifferent to some, but I had no idea how gentle, yet protective, God was to me. The Enemy was after my soul and wanted to destroy not just me, but my blessed seed, my daughter. God put something in me, and He put something in my daughter. It was a purpose that can only be birthed through the Revelation of knowing Him first. Countless times I've been given the privilege of knowing the gifts in someone else. I got to show them what was necessary for God to take them to the next step. It is truly a planned thing to say what the Holy Spirit is saying to those, bringing darkness into the light.

Again, it may sound unusual, but I wasn't brought up in a church that operated in the gifts of the Spirit, even though I went to church. It didn't learn anything from the church, except how to be religious. Well, that was only the beginning. God began His work in me right away. I began to feel different about a lot of things, I was even a better person in many ways. I learned to respond to a love I had never known before, with so many questions that still needed to be answered. I liked the idea of going to church, as to belong somewhere, but as I found myself thinking: "I'm somewhat out of place." It was as though the people there did not want to accept me. Little did I know: some were hidden killers. This explains *John 16:2*, which is still hard to believe at times. People in church will do this to others, who in their minds are not Kingdom worthy. Maybe God did not reveal me to you because I will be used as a deliverer, but you decided to try and take me out before my time: NOT SO!

As I kept going to church, I would look around at all these people, who would look like they were praying. They acted holy, with uplifted hands, and I would ask God, "Why am I here? What am I doing here with all these holy people, doing what they are doing?"

Much to my surprise, He showed me what I didn't know, but needed to know. One day, He told me to "look again." As I did, He opened my spiritual eyes for a glimpse. It took me by surprise because I did not see people, I saw the Spirits in people—and they did not look like God at all. It was quite alarming to me, and it was only for a few moments. I shuddered inside, because I could not believe what I was seeing.

The spirit realm opened to me, and I saw for the first time what He meant as He would tell me: "Be careful." It was beyond my own natural perception for the first time. Here, I had been thinking all along, I was not worthy to be there. Suddenly, God was revealing to me what was around me. Do not be surprised by this: those who teach or preach the Word do not want an uprising in their church, so they avoid many things that should be made known. God wants His people to know these things. It is called spiritual insight: to know who are the wheat and who are the tares, what is God and what is not God.

I began to go from not knowing anything at all to the amazing revelation of the Spirit Realm, and yes, it is real! People have a body, we have a soul, and we have a spirit. Now the question is: what kind of spirit do you have? Until you are saved, you are open to becoming influenced or tricked by The Enemy into thinking you are with them—and not a child of God. You still must accept Jesus Christ as your Savior and Lord. However, also remember it is The Enemy who is after you and would rather you be dead then ever make it to your purpose. When you come into the Kingdom, well, now you have an even bigger target on your back. The Adversary knows you will be taught the Word, and begin to gain knowledge of who he is, and how he thinks about killing you.

One night, I was especially alarmed. I was startled in my sleep in the middle of the night by a heavy spiritual presence. It came very close to my face, as if it were sitting on my chest and breathing with horrible breath. I was frozen, and I tried to grasp my bearings to try and understand what was going on. I could not move, and all I had thought to do was say the name of Jesus. I kept thinking: "What is this thing, and how did it get so close to me?" I wanted it to leave and go away, never to come back again. Finally, I said, "Jesus, help me!" and before I knew it, that thing was gone. It was sent to make me afraid, and it did for a time, because I didn't understand why it showed up in the first place. I was determined to find out. So, I began to ask the questions. Just be careful who you ask, because not everyone has the spiritual knowledge to give you the right answer. There were times I would ask someone at church different questions, only to find out they did not have any clue. They just had a badge.

In other words, they dismissed my experience as if it has never happened, because these things had not happened to them. They are not a threat to the Kingdom of Darkness. You will not pose a threat to The Enemy if you do not truly study the Word to gain any revelation. If you do not have revelation, especially *Luke 4:4* and *Luke 10:19*: "And Jesus answered him, saying, 'It is written, that man shall not live by bread alone, but by every Word of God.'" "Behold, I give unto you power to tread on serpents and scorpions and over all the power of The Enemy; and nothing shall by any means hurt you." You will not be a threat at first, but the moment you become one, The Enemy begins another strategy to work the evil he has planned for you. Why? Because he now knows that you know what you did not know before.

The next time I went to church, I explained to one of the ushers what happened to me. I was escorted to an office of an assistant to one of the pastors, who told me it was a demonic presence sent to scare me. This woman's name was Mary, and I was totally unaware of her purpose in this ministry. I just knew she was giving me insight that would help me along the way. She said I did the right thing by saying the name of Jesus, who gives us authority over demons when they manifest like that. Well, I was a babe in Christ, and quite disturbed by all this. I knew nothing, absolutely nothing about the Spirit Realm, and was forced to learn rather quickly, because they kept coming. Not every night, but many times after this, I would find myself facing a presence I knew was not Jesus. This was all very new to me. What I was being taught at each service wasn't helping me with what was happening in the middle of the night. Oh, if people who wear the badges at church would be more equipped so they could be a help, instead of being know-it-alls.

As I was growing up, all I really knew about church was going on Sunday morning and coming home to have a treat with my family. My father would prepare us a drink with half coffee and half milk to dunk our Sunday donuts in. We only prayed at the evening meal. There was never a Bible mentioned or Bible verses ever spoken. We did not say the name of Jesus at all; we just didn't. Sometimes my mother would talk about angels. I guess that is why she would call me one, but she knew what she could not say.

We went to a Catholic school and even in our catechism class there was nothing but sheer nonsense. We did not even open the Bible to be taught anything. It truly was the blind leading the blind, to keep us blind, until I asked God one day: "Who are you"? Yes, we all need to ask Him this.

I really wanted to know Him, and He took me on a journey I will never forget! I began having so many spiritual encounters throughout each week, leading up to Sunday, I really thought something was wrong with me. These spirits would manifest in my room at night, and I would just freeze. I had not come to the Revelation I had the power and authority over the spirits who would come to taunt me. There were different kinds. Those who came, came in many forms. I hated going to bed at night. I am quite sure I am not the only one this has happened to: it's just my story being told here. Speak up and tell someone about it, because it is going on and people need to know. Most people do not know who to talk to when this happens. I had just became born again. I did not want anyone to know something was wrong with me, I wanted someone to help me understand. spiritual warfare is no joke, but why would this happen to me so soon? The Devil doesn't care what you think, he just doesn't want you to know you have the authority to rebuke and stop him. Pick up your Bible and read the Word, so you can find out for yourself how to handle these demonic spirits.

Believe me, this was a very unsettling place to be in, before knowing who God said I am. I knew the name of Jesus; however, I honestly did not understand or have the Revelation of how much power He gives us as His children. No one bothered to tell me. Even as I was going through this process of becoming aware the Spirit Realm was real, God used me in other ways, also. He told me I was His, and He was preparing me for something great. I remember a few months later, I had a dream about this same woman named Mary. Yes, she was an assistant to a pastor in the church, but this was something totally different.

You see, God will use who He chooses to bring about an awareness to someone, even if they have been in ministry much longer than you. It doesn't matter: she needed to know what God was showing me. The dream was about her and in the dream, she had an opening under her arm (where the armpit would be) as if it were a birthing canal, instead of where it is normally located. She was ready to give birth, but it wasn't from the normal channel. God was letting me know I had the gift to interpret dreams. This was the first of many gifts God gave me.

Thinking I was doing the right thing, I went to visit her on my own, unannounced. I was unsure of myself, like a little kitten. I knocked, and she answered the door and invited me in. We sat. Mary was studying the Word of God, but was very gracious to me. I began to tell her of the dream, and it seemed to alarm her at first. I'm sure she may have been thinking: "Why would God use Rebecca to have a dream and come to tell me about it?"

Well, He had given me the gift of knowing dreams and interpreting them. It's an amazing gift, and I have had many since that time, helping others to understand theirs as well as understanding my own. I do pray first, not depending on my own ability. It is a gift of God. He gives it as another way to speak to us. It was also given so she would know I have this gift.

After we spoke a little, I left, but was very unsure of how this would affect our relationship at church. At the time, I was still young in the Lord, as some would consider, but I just knew I had to tell her about the dream. Many months later, I understood the reason for the dream was prophetic: to help Mary know she was going to birth a spiritual baby, but it was not going to come the way she thought it would. God used me to give her a revelation about it. I did not fully understand this gift of interpreting dreams, but I knew I had it. God was going to use it to speak to me and others along the way. Of course, keep in mind, because I was just a babe in Christ, people didn't want to believe. God will use you, He does. In other words, to make it plain, God uses those who He knows will respond, no matter how long you have attended church. God was letting those around me know I was special, and even though they did not want to accept it, it was all right to be who He said I am—and not who they thought I was. It's so sad, because people undermine others as if to say what they think it more important than what God has said. I continued to think something was wrong with me, so instead of becoming bold for Christ, I became introverted. I thought I needed the approval of men. You could just see it, as if to say: "Who in the heck did I think I was, to tell them anything?"

So many get caught up in titles given to them, they miss the whole purpose of the reason they are in position in the first place. It is not about the title, it's about being there because God put you there to be a help, not a hindrance, in the work of His Kingdom. You can be born again one moment and behind the pulpit preaching and teaching the Gospel the next. Who is to say, but God?

You can be an usher (or porter, as they were called in the Old Testament), and do more for God's Kingdom because the promotion was given to you by the Lord. When you read *Psalm 75:6*: "This Word expresses to those who considered themselves promoted by man's standards. I would much rather be an usher or a greeter in the House of God with an anointing, than to be a pastor who teaches the Word without the presence of God."

God is not concerned about people's opinions, He wants them to get the information, using whomever, by any means possible. Yet, at the same time, reveal something to someone, so they may know about the person God is using. I do not know if she dismissed this or not, but I do know it came from the Lord. He gave it to me to speak to her. Do not be afraid of men, only fear the Lord. Amen!

So, when the Word says out of the mouth of babes (*Matthew 11:25, 21:16*), it does not necessarily mean a young person. I believe it means someone with an innocence of Christ, so when they speak, people will know this is of the Lord. They could not have known the information any other way, but by God. That is why He chooses the foolish things, because in innocence they go forth without fear and deliver the Word of truth. A prophetic word of authenticity can't be messed up and be misinterpreted by someone who is full of themselves. This is what happens many times with people who think they are called, rather than God calling them, and it ends up being pride, and not a gift that He can use.

When I pray, I am very sincere about those I am praying for. The prayers coming out of my mouth make me realize God uses prayers to bring His Glory right into my home. I remember I was praying for my pastor and his wife one morning. As I finished, I opened my eyes and saw this beautiful blue-like haze in my kitchen. I said to God: "Well, this is new." He responded: It is My Glory. The prayer you just prayed so pleased me My Presence came in to let you know."

This is how it is supposed to be in church. God wants to take up habitation, but He is only allowed visitation in ninety percent of churches. If there would be true intercessors in the church praying in the sanctuary, and those in the choir who can touch Heaven with not just a song, but actual worship before the pastor brings the Word, God would manifest His presence in a greater measure. We are His chosen, and so much more. We become the holy vessels for the Lord to work through. The Glory Cloud comes to reign in habitation, not visitation. This is why the worship team, and the intercessors, all must know how to operate in the gifts. They must work together each time we come together to welcome His Presence in our churches. He will not just come, he will stay. Are you ready to work for the Lord like this, and create an atmosphere for healing and deliverance to be common-place in your church? Then this is the way to do it!

I John 2:27 says: "But the anointing, which ye have received of Him abideth in you, and ye need not that any man teach you; but as the same anointing teacheth you of all things, and is truth, and is no lie, and even as it hath taught you, ye shall abide in Him."

This is how I learned what I know, because I sought after God to know these things. I did not wait for man to try and give me an explanation. I wanted to know for myself who God is, and He allowed me in.

You know, it is rather funny. My sister did not come to visit me for one year after I had bought my first home. When she did finally come to pay a visit, she came in the front door. While looking around, she asked if I had purchased new furniture. I replied: "No, not at all." The Lord was revealing to me it wasn't any new furniture, it was His Presence that made the difference. The Lord had brought her to my home for her to know me as the new creature in Christ, no longer the simple Becky she'd grown up with. I was becoming who God called me to be. She only knew to identify it as new furniture, but the atmosphere had changed in my home because He had taken up habitation. Oh, Glory to God! I would love that all would develop a relationship with the Holy Spirit and have Him present in your house. The Enemy knows who has power through revelation and who doesn't. Make sure you are one that knows!

<u>An encounter with The Enemy!</u>

One night, as I was just getting ready to go to sleep, I felt a huge thud on the roof of my townhome which was right above my bedroom. It frightened me. I thought: "What the heck was that?" You would never expect anything like that to happen. I just decided to fall asleep anyway, knowing whatever it was, God would somehow take care of it.

Well, to my surprise, as God showed me a few years later, it was a demon who tried to scare me. It somehow manifested into our realm and landed on my roof—only to find out a few minutes later, a huge sword-yielding angel of God came and commanded that demon to leave. I don't know why these things happen, they just do. I needed to know God was with me, and He is My Protector and Provider. Wherever God was taking me, and whatever it was He had for me, something was already trying to stop it. Perhaps this was supposed to give me confidence in who Jesus is, and help me discern spiritual things happening around me. It still took years of prayer and understanding. For all I was shown, with so much information to know, it did not deter me wanting more. Until I could see through my spiritual eyes, He was allowing me to know what I needed to know about the current place I was in. God never gives you more than you are ready to understand, until you can handle it. As you grow more fully in the things of God and in His ways, you are given insight into greater things. We do not need to even inquire about some things until it is time to understand them.

I must say, I cried most of the way through things, because no one would believe God was using me the way He did. I wanted to tell people, but when they would give me that look and dismiss me so incredibly quickly without thinking twice. It would thrust yet another thorn in my heart instead of encouraging me. I honestly would think: "Why is God not using them like this?." As time went on, He would show me, they are not interested in what God could do through them. They just wanted their own recognition, from the title they were sporting. These are the ones who become an unwilling vessel to God, because they want the glory of what they are doing. When you stay humble, God will exalt you in due season for others to see, right under their noses.

This brings me to the time God decided to show me another way He would use me outside the four walls of a church. I went to the cleaners to pick up my dry cleaning. As I rounded the corner into the plaza where the dry cleaner was located, I noticed of group of men lined up next to their motorcycles. As I drew closer to them, I could tell they were looking at me while I parked. It was a quickening in my spirit, but I did not know how God was going to use me.

When I finished my business inside the dry-cleaning store, I heard the Lord speak to me and say: "Go tell them about Jesus." This meant I had to walk about 200 steps to where those men were standing, and explain I was sent to tell them about Jesus. I cringed because I did not like how they were looking at me in the first place. But hesitantly, I did what the Lord told me to do. I came up to them, seeing they were more desirous of my flesh. I asked if any of them know who Jesus was. As I opened my mouth, one by one they all walked away from me without saying a word. They all gave me looks like, "Who the heck does this lady think she is?" Well, as they departed, the Holy Ghost whirled me around and opened my mouth, and pointed to one man in particular. He said to this man: "Something is going to happen to you, and you are going to remember you rejected my daughter this day. Just as you have rejected her, I will reject you, because she is sent by God to you." The man just stared at me, not willing to move at all. Then, as I looked to my left, one man elevated his hands and lifted them in the air. What was meant to be said was spoken. I am a true prophet of God, but we are not all used the same. Many times, we are sent to those who will not make it to a church. I just kept walking because the message had been delivered!

CHAPTER EIGHT

Funny, now that I look back: when I would go to church on Sundays and Wednesdays, all I did was mimic what I saw other people doing. It was all I knew to do. I wasn't filled with the Spirit yet, and able to worship God the way I should. I think many people start out that way, wondering: "Why am I doing this?" or "Am I in the right place?." I don't know. Maybe it was just me.

You must understand, I had never seen a choir like that singing praises to a God. I had not seen people lifting their hands in the air, high above their heads. It was like asking myself: "What is really going on here?" I wanted to know what it all meant. I started out by lifting my hands just enough to show they were up, but not all the way. However, each week, my hands began to lift higher and higher as I became more and more aware of why I was doing it. Sometimes I would come to church out of obligation, just like I did when I went to church as a Catholic. Yet, the change was being done inside me, as God kept drawing me. He was doing the work in me. I felt different, yet I did not understand why I felt the way I did. Even as I was taught about the tithe, I had to give according to what my faith was ready to give. I was raising my daughter on my own, so her needs came first. However, little by little, my giving increased. I became a full tither sooner than I thought. I took my time, and did not allow the pastor to manipulate the Word of God, saying I must be a tither to be blessed by God. He was already blessing me in many ways even before I came to church!

After one year of going to church, I came home one Sunday. I asked God: "What is wrong with me?" I would see people come together as a family unit. They would come in, sit together, pray together, and praise together, but that wasn't happening for me. All God said was "Nothing!"

I wanted my family to come to know Jesus in this way, but my natural father would tell me: "Rebecca, you are welcome to come here to visit us anytime you want, just don't talk about Jesus."

I couldn't believe my ears, and I would tell him, "But Dad, you would be surprised how many people want to know Him." In other words, "Why don't you want to know about Him?" It was very frustrating. They were trying to get me to come back to Catholicism, but I had found the Jesus who was no longer on the cross. I was not going back, and I really liked where the Lord was leading me, even though I did not always understand where He was going. I just needed the time to get to know God at my pace, and know I was not just a child of God, but that He has purpose for my life. I needed to be willing to walk it and find out what I needed to know.

Much to my surprise, I was visiting my father one afternoon. We were sitting in the living room, when suddenly, I felt the room become very still and quiet. Before I knew what was happening, my dad started to lean over on his side and say to me: "Don't you pray for me, don't you pray for me!" Then, up out of my belly, I said this without realizing it: "The Lord rebuke you, Satan!"

My father jerked within himself and that was that. The religious Spirit in him left because the Holy Ghost said so. I was excited, yet still afraid of what would happen next. Every day, it seemed something was happening. No one at my church knew I had this great gift inside me, and I didn't know what to do with it. There was literally no one to ask. I had to walk this journey myself and make decisions for myself for the first time: steps in my life as a born-again believer. spiritual gifts are for God to teach you what man cannot teach you. They only think they can, so do not rely on the knowledge they give. Always get a first opinion, which is asking the Holy Ghost. He will discern through your spirit what is true and what isn't, and show you exactly how to proceed.

After something like this would happen, the Lord kept implying to me there was really nothing wrong with me. It was His way of assuring me I was all right, and that He was doing this for His Glory. I was in training, still trying to comprehend what each thing meant. What He meant by nothing being wrong with me was eventually made known:

it was the spirit in them. They did not like the Holy Spirit living in me. You see, the wheat grew up with the tare, we are in the field together because the seed of enemy was planted while men slept. This parable is found in *Matthew 13:24-30*.

People in church were hateful, jealous, unkind, and rude. The whole time I would be thinking: "Well, I don't want to end up like that." Being a babe in Christ was causing me to ask more questions than I had answers for. Especially when I would ask them the questions no one else would dare to ask.

I really did not want to become what I saw. But alas, instead of distancing myself, I kept trying to fit in. God did not want that. He wanted me to become what He had called me out of the darkness for. God was keeping me separate from those who did not understand what He was taking me through. They would have thwarted every move of God in my life, if given the chance, including my own family. I loved my family very much, and wanted them to love Jesus the way I was beginning to. There is a time for everyone to come into the Kingdom and understand what Jesus did for each one of us on the cross. However, until you take that first step, you will never know the plans God has for you.

I remember a time when the Lord spoke to me and said: "Rebecca, your family is saved. They just do not want to serve me the way you do." I knew then it just was not time for them to understand what God was doing in my life. I had to make the decision to keep moving forward, while walking with God alone.

This recalls to my mind the Revelation I received while listening to a pastor preach on salvation. He ministered: "Unless the Holy Ghost draws them, they won't come." In other words, the Holy Spirit is always ministering to those who are being made ready for the invitation to be saved. It is an invitation, and then a knowing to acknowledge and accept. We must be patient while waiting for the preparation of the heart to receive this. Each one who is called for salvation will respond at the appointed time.

One day, when I came to visit my dad on a Sunday afternoon with all my other siblings there, I was sitting in the living room reading the paper. One by one, my family kept coming in to ask me to join them on the front lawn. It was a beautiful day, but very warm. After the third time, I finally put down the paper and went outside to sit with my family and just talk or "visit", as my dad would call it. Very soon a breeze came through and my father said to me: "Oh sure, as soon as you come out, here comes the nice wind we needed." This meant God waited until I came to join them for all to enjoy His breath of fresh air. The Lord will make it known to you, even if others do not understand what they should know, but have not yet asked for. I was a very curious child of God, and I wanted to know everything I could.

I know God uses many ways to get our attention when He is telling us about Himself. My story of what happened to me during these occurrences will surely be a blessing to others, as they read and interpret it was the Holy Spirit who will bring about an explanation for what may have happened to you. So, if those who are reading this book will take a moment to contemplate some things you may have been wondering, but did not ask, now is the time.

I have tried to write as many things as possible about my life, but there is so much more to tell. What He has done for me, and what He will do for you, can be amazing if you take the time to ask. Then wait to hear the answer. Are you curious enough to know what God has for you?

In *John 21:25*, the last scripture in this book of John, it says: "And there are so many other things which Jesus did, the which, if they should be written everyone, I suppose that even the world itself could not contain the books that should be written. Amen." When I read this verse it makes me think about all the things God has done for me, to become aware of who He is. Yes, I am special to the Lord and loved unconditionally, but that does not mean I am excluded in the Revelation of the kind of love God has for each one of us. It is in the seeking after the introduction that allows us to know about our Creator.

I know there are many who will not want or desire salvation. For myself, I will not take the risk of thinking: "What would have happened to me, had I not accepted the invitation when it came?"

It's a privilege to know my soul will be carried to Heaven by the holy angels of God when my time here on Earth comes to an end, and that I will live on forever with God. That's an amazing thought, because most people are so busy living here, they forget there is also an eternity to consider.

Have you thought about yours?

CHAPTER NINE

I honestly believed what I heard from preachers only about forty percent of the time when I went to church, especially when they spoke about the money we were supposed to give. I was not convinced at all about what I was hearing versus what I was experiencing during this walk of faith I was on. It was different every day and very frustrating because I had no prayer partner to encourage me. I was always by myself. So, I had to engage every day, starting with prayer, and trusting in God to lead me and tell me what His Word meant to me and for me. Or at least that's what I thought. He was watching over me, trying to keep me from being hurt any more than I had already been. The behavior of those who thought they were superior only had a badge with a title that did not line up with God's Word, so I was not impressed at all by what I saw or what I heard. From Sunday to Wednesday, and then from Wednesday to Sunday, I witnessed many things. So, I had to learn to discern what was the truth, apply it to my own life, and trust the Lord. The thing that bothered me most: there was no one to really ask, as I would get twenty different responses for the same question. So, I just stopped asking. This is the place where God said: "Ask Me, get to know who I AM." He had an answer to my every question.

How was I to know all those people did not have a real relationship with the Lord outside the four walls of the church building? They couldn't give me an intelligent answer. I assumed because they had a badge, they would respond with something I could grasp. Instead I'd get a look, and they'd say: "That doesn't happen to me." Or: "Why would God talk to you like that?"

I came to find out it was nothing more than their fleshly opinion, and not a true response by the Holy Ghost. I have come to know there are not many who even know who the Holy Ghost really is. Oh yes, it's true. Just because someone sits beside you at church does not mean they are there to learn the Bible or to know God. Quick frankly, this is how The Enemy would make me feel rejection, and try to minimize what God was saying to me, even more than I already felt. People would come sit next to me at church and suddenly just get up and move to another seat. I took it as rejection, but God showed me it was His Presence around me that would cause them to get up and leave. I just didn't know it yet! It's the spirit in them, not the spirit in you.

You must want to know Jesus and love Him, not to just get saved, and walk around as if you know Him.

You will be able to discern quicker than you realize when you just ask God. The Word in *John 8:32* says: "And they shall know the truth and the truth will set them free."

There comes a time as you walk with Him when you will know *John 8:36:* "And whom the Son sets free is free indeed." It's called a progression in your relationship with the Father, and it takes time if you are willing to invest in Him. You begin to learn more and more as the Lord shows you what is going around you. You do not have to be friends with everyone to be accepted: just know the one Friend you will always need. His name is Jesus, and what a friend He can be. Do not miss what God has for you by serving man, instead of serving Him.

I guess everyone else was too caught up in their own recognition to even think God was desiring to use me. It's amazing how He will hide you from those who would try to harm you, while He is preparing you for work He has ahead of you. I just had yet to keep discovering His way.

Little by little, or you could say, line upon line, precept upon precept, I was learning all I needed to know by the Holy Spirit, who patiently took the time to assure me of my guaranteed walk was good. I took one day at a time and began to walk with God on my own, allowing myself to be led. I didn't always know what I was doing or why, so I just began to ask the One who would know. As He would speak to me, it was startling many times. God, the creator of Heaven and Earth was talking to me, inviting me into a place I was learning all about. Wow! I wanted to know: "Why do I need to do all these things, instead of getting the conflicting information from those I thought would be able to answer me?" As I grew in the knowledge of the Word, faith began to arise in me. I saw how God was helping me see the things I needed to know through His eyes. It only made me think about the plans He had for me. What were those plans? Even though people treated me like I was just stupid and insignificant along the way, I kept desiring to know what He was telling me about each one and each thing I encountered: not what people perceived or thought. It still hurt in many ways, because I was still vulnerable to the looks, the jeers, and the sneers from people in church. I thought they loved God, but all they did was love the title there were given by men. I did not even want to talk to anyone at church or even bother with them. It was like going to school, but learning from a different teacher: not the one in front of you, but the One inside of you.

I went through a time of tale-bearing at the church, an Old Testament term for gossip, in case you do not know what the term means. I would see people walking down the hallway towards me at church. As they would see me, they would engage in a conversation with each other, just so they would not have to speak to me. This was not the church God described to me at all! The Holy Spirit covered my ears so as not to hear what they were saying about me, because if I had, it would have destroyed me. This is how caring the Lord is. When He has a specific purpose for you, He will protect you at all costs, regardless of what people are doing or saying. It was alarming how others could think so highly of themselves, and at the same time not have good things to say about others. Yes, it began to irritate me to the point I hated going to church, even though I was supposed to be there. In other words, they thought they had arrived, and I was not even worthy to be there. I wanted to prove it to all of them, so I remember asking God to have me take some giant steps. As I took one step, I realized there were a lot of things I was not prepared for. I backed up quickly. I told the Lord how sorry I was for asking Him to oblige me in my own way, to show others that I counted and mattered to God. That's the flesh side of a person, not the Spirit, but I was learning.

It's amazing how God will use the very one others think are not worthy in their own eyes or perception, and move them along rather quickly to get them into the position the other person was trying to hold them back from, or they would never be considered for. Even though they would not include me, God never excluded me. I was always welcome in His loving arms, and I fell into them many times. "Believe Me!" God was speaking to me and showing me things in a way even I could not believe sometimes. It was always about the church: what He thought about His church and how He wanted His church to be. I would ask God: "What can I do about it, or why?" Because I really didn't think there was anything I could do about it. He was using me inside the church many times, by not even responding to those who would never accept me. God was making a loud statement to those around me: "I chose Rebecca, not you."

He was showing me the difference between man's version of the church and His vision for the church. Even though I wanted so much to be accepted in God's House, no one would believe what God was revealing to me. So, I continued to just learn as I went. I wanted to shout it from the rooftops: "He loves me, He really loves me!" and I still do to this day. In my quiet time with the Lord, He holds me in His loving arms, and lets me know every day how much I am valued and needed by Him. No matter how much rejection you endure, it does not mean you are off the list for God to use. It is only preparation in progress.

I did everything by myself. I was getting used to it. Being a human being, we want to be accepted by others, but it is many times for our own benefit to be alone while the Holy Spirit ministers to us. This is how God showed me what people do, standing right there with inviting arms open wide. I remember going to a Safeway store. As I came up to order some turkey and cheese slices for sandwiches from the deli counter, I noticed the young lady at the counter was helping someone else already. I waited my turn. She looked at me for a moment, then just turned and walked away, as if I had not been standing there at all. Another clerk at the counter then came to help me. I am sure my look was enough to say: "Did she not even see me standing there?" As I left the counter, I could feel the presence of the Lord, and He said: "This is what My people do to Me every day, Rebecca. I reveal Myself to them, they look at Me for a moment, and then just turn to walk away, when My arms are open wide to them."

Honestly, I stopped for a moment because it made tears well up in my eyes. I thought: "How could people not want Jesus?" He was so good to me, with His loving ways and gentle ways towards me when others would just brush me off so quickly. I knew I was His child, and He would use me to bring others into His Kingdom. I just knew it!

God will take His time with you, so as you are given knowledge of the Kingdom, you will know how to be responsible with what He gives you, when He gives it to you. To whom much is given, much is required in *Luke 12:48.* The Lord showed me that before I was even ready to do any work in or out of His church. Being used by God is a responsibility, because there are souls at stake here. Jesus was given those souls from God to nurture, protect, and keep. I find those in church quickly drop so many people because they think we are not important, but the Lord sees things differently.

As always, wanting to be included rather than excluded, I invited someone from the current church I was attending to my home. I thought it would be good to get to know some of the people I fellowshipped and volunteered with. Even in doing what would seem a normal invitation can be disastrous when you invite without asking God first. I thought it innocent enough, but the person already had a predetermined conclusion about who I was before I even realized it.

The woman informed me, just out of the blue, after only being in my home less than an hour: "You need to be more thankful about the job you have."

I quickly responded, "Why should I be thankful, I'm doing all the work?" I answered as honestly as I felt. I was upset by the question, because it was really none of her business. Her attempt to make me feel bad about something good He had blessed me with hurt me. I was given this great job, and I had worked for the company for almost eighteen years at that time. The truth was, I was grateful for what I had accomplished, being a single mother. I just did not know that I needed to give thanks every single day, the same way others did. So, to end this chapter, let's just say God gives everyone a learning curve to know Him, as we mature in the knowledge of who He is. When people press you for information, make sure you are responding with the love of God, for all intended purposes, to answer every man who asks when they ask, even if it is a foolish question. I was not aware of the evil intent behind the question of jealousy in the first place. I just answered it as I knew how to respond. My innocent thinking was undermined, but I had to keep moving forward, no matter what occurred. I was so disappointed most of the time, because I needed and wanted to interact with others, but seeing how it turned out each time, I just stopped.

I continued to have many questions, such as: "Why do people say things like Praise the Lord so much without any meaning in the expression?" I did not feel the depth of compassion on what they said. Why, when someone would say: "God Bless You", would you feel as if a knife just cut through you instead of an actual blessing? I began to ask: "Why am I hearing prayers from those who sound so poetic, yet are actually so empty? Why was I supposed to be reading my Bible every day, or going to church twice a week?"

I soon discovered it was much more than I had ever considered before. The spiritual side of Rebecca was beginning to know her God, much quicker and with more ease than the ones I knew at church. It was not because I was better, I was just persistent in finding out who I was and what I was desiring to know for my future: which was to be a leader and not a follower.

I learned not to have church people come to my home anymore after that. I did not have to explain myself to anyone about anything, I just wanted to be accepted without blame or defining myself. I found this to be impossible with most church-goers, because all they do is go to church. Apparently, no one at this place had the maturity to identify with me, or to understand who I was in Christ. This is what they call a superficial relationship with God: it is surface, not a transformation. As you read in *II Timothy 3:5*: "Having a form of godliness, but denying the power thereof; from such turn away." This is what most people have while going to church, because they are afraid to allow the Holy Spirit an internal view of themselves. He will show them what needs to change on the inside. If they would allow God in, then the true Christian would come out—not a false one showing the flesh instead of the Spirit.

Don't shipwreck someone just because you do not understand what God is doing in them. It was truly amazing how the Holy Spirit was so real in me, and how He would intervene when I didn't know what to do at all. It's called showing, revealing, and teaching. This method of learning allows you to go home and read the Word, so we will grow in the knowledge of God. I have come to know many of us who God chooses to use will be home-schooled, rather than allow people at church to try and help us understand what only God can reveal. If you are not spirit-filled, you will come to our aide with a quick assessment, a quick conclusion, and an even quicker dismissal. Most just do not understand the work going on in someone, because it is God working in them. Many do not realize we are the ones God will raise up to be mighty men and mighty women of Faith, and will be used to ensure others come forward also. It is so important to ask God for the discerning of the Holy Ghost, so you can be a helper in the Kingdom, not a hindrance.

One night, as I was getting ready for bed, I had a round vanilla scented candle with three wicks sitting on a table stand next to my bed. I lit the candles, turned out the lights, and lay there, trying to fall asleep. Suddenly, I felt a quick breeze come through my bedroom and I heard: "I'm coming, I'm coming, I'm coming!" and then it was quiet. I knew something was going to happen and I was being prepared for it. I went to sleep with expectation.

Maybe a month later, He just came in, without an announcement. It was the manifestation of God's Spirit in my room, there to heal my heart from all the afflictions I had suffered. My personal encounter with God began to heal a broken Spirit so tenderly as only He could.

I was sitting in my bedroom, in front of a vanity table by myself, when suddenly the atmosphere changed. I knew the Spirit of God was there in my room, hovering over me. I was not frightened at all, and I just sat still.

I did not move. I remained calm because I knew it was the Lord holding me close. It was time for my heart to go through a spiritual surgery, and He was the surgeon. It was as if I knew what was happening to me, although I was awake I was in His realm and in His operating room. He began to do what I know only the Holy Spirit could perform. He was showing me I had many thorns that had been thrust in my heart over the last forty years. He was removing them one by one. Some were large and some were small, but there were forty of them. As He took each one of them out of my heart, I was shown the moment they went in. As each thorn left my heart, I would feel a slight prick. Every thorn had a name: who had done this to me and why. It was so amazing. The feeling was incredibly tender and loving, even though the thorns were meant to destroy me. One thorn, in particular, was very large. He removed it with such great gentleness and care. He began to maneuver it out ever so slightly to ensure it would not do any damage to my heart. Now, I know not everyone will have this God kind of supernatural, internal healing, but He heard my cry and I desired to worship my King. It was the event that took place for me to sing and to love my God the way He created me to.

It seemed to take a long duration of time, but there was nothing more than the love of my Father and the gentleness of His skillful hand as He was pulling them out, not to amaze me, but to shower me with the care He wanted to give me. He would gently pull a thorn backwards, and would stop with each centimeter because it was very close to a major artery, so as not to damage my heart while it was being removed. I'm sure this procedure went on for a good while. When He was finished, I could feel Him begin to leave my room. It was all so surreal. I know it was for me to experience God in a way only I could benefit from this beautiful display of love.

He let me know to close my eyes and rest for what He had come to do was complete. I crawled into my bed and slept like a baby. When I woke up, it was a new day for me. I felt so good inside and could not wait to get to church that morning. I wanted to praise the Lord, because all the obstructions had been removed the night before. Nothing preventing me from opening my heart to give Him the praise He waited a long time to hear. Can you imagine God loving you that much!

I sang praises to my God and King like never before, because all the blockage had been removed. I had a new heart, and I had been released to worship Him. I wanted everyone to know what God had done for me, but found no one wanted to even know. I guess it would be my secret for many years: the amazing was our Heavenly Father thinks about us. When it seems no one else really cares, He does!

How would I ever begin to explain to anybody what had happened to me that night? Who would ever believe it? This is one of the reasons I decided to write my story. I want people to know God is so much more than you could ever even begin to think. When God calls you and He needs to prepare a vessel for His Glory, He will perform the doing of it. It is truly up to us to cooperate, even though we may not even know what it is just yet or how it will happen. Just believe!

I specifically chose this verse to put in the front of my book as a testament to the Lord: "For I know the thoughts I think towards you, saith the Lord, thoughts of peace and not of evil to give you hope and an expected end," found in *Jeremiah 29:11.*" The Lord will give you hints along the way as He shows you how to love, to correct, to redeem, to vindicate, to justify, to warn, to teach, to protect, to provide, to ensure, to allow, to never give up, and to trust.

Please take the time to read *Isaiah 43:1-2*, then turn your eyes to read *Isaiah 45:1-9*. These overlooked passages in the Word of God will bring answers to your internal heart's questions that have remained unknown or unanswered to you and others until now. It is time for revelation; it just is!

God called me out of darkness into His marvelous light, and He speaks these words to me as the memory of that day comes back with a quickening in my spirit, as if it were yesterday. Many have mocked me, or decided I was not worthy to be a minister of the Gospel. But He has assured me, I am chosen for this purpose. He is the reason I needed to tell my story!

"For the Spirit of the Lord God is upon me; because the Lord hath anointed me to preach good tidings unto the meek; He hath sent me to bind up the brokenhearted, to proclaim liberty to the captives, and the opening of the prison to them that are bound." *Isaiah 61:1*

CHAPTER TEN

As each one of my siblings began noticing the change in me, they questioned why I was so interested in going to church. I had not really shown that I desired to attend church, except when forced to go to appease my parents. Their thoughts and my course in what I believed were all changing, concerning a religious perception of what being a Catholic was in this new spiritual awareness I'd found in God.

They thought I had become obsessed with a motivated time and course He had me on. Well, it wasn't an obsession, it was a revelation. They had the wrong information concerning who they thought I was, based on us growing up together. In fact, to them I was just their sister: nothing more, nothing less. But I knew differently. It was the story of Joseph, being played out in my family, from a woman's view. God chose me anyway. It's only a matter of time before God will show them who their sister really has become. He made a way for me, but it was for their benefit.

The only difference was I responding to the voice and leading of the Holy Spirit, now that I was born again. My spirit was adjusting to God so quickly, and I was beginning to know Him more and more each day. They did the same thing to Jesus, asking the question: "Isn't this Joseph's son?" In other words, who does anyone think they are when they step forward and be who God called us to be, even out from our own families?

Those in the synagogues, when Jesus was just beginning His ministry and becoming known to the Pharisees and scribes, thought the Son of God wasn't important. After all, they had been coming to the synagogue longer with their fine robes and eloquent speech. Who was this man who thought He could disregard them, only speaking to sinners and ignoring their position? In *Luke 7:49*, they asked: "Who was this man?" But God did not call the righteous, He called sinners to repentance. So, their self-righteous attitudes only meant they did not think they needed a savior.

I am sure many of you out there have experienced the same thing in your families. Suddenly, we are saved, and then our character is attacked. They know us as the person we were before we knew Christ, not after. It's what I call B.C. (Before Christ) instead of A.D (After Death). I just knew I was changing, and my mind was set to be who God said I am, rather than stay where I was. It is an awakening in Spirit to begin to think, walk, and even to talk like we should as children of the King.

As I continued to go to church, I started experiencing more and more spiritual things. I wanted answers. I did not realize that those who made themselves look important at church really did not know God at all. They would explain it away by saying: "I've been coming to this church for twenty years, and He doesn't say such things to me. Why would God talk to you like He does?" It just goes to show you, people are not who they claim to be because of a badge.

They were referring to how young I was in my walk, as if God only spoke to certain ones. He speaks when he desires to speak to His children, if they are interested in what He has to say. I did not have anyone to ask what was going on outside of being there, because the people in the church would not respond to my questions with an answer coming from the Spirit. I knew the difference, even if they did not. I would just say okay and walk away bewildered, because I thought they were supposed to know. As I began to pursue what I was looking for, I realized these people really did not know God at all, even though they acted like they did. Putting on these famous acts, like the Pharisees and the Scribes, would try to make people think they were holy. It was a pretense of what I was actually experiencing. People would come to church just for others to see what car they drove or how beautiful the dress they had on looked.

I was quite sick of the façade I was seeing each time I entered the sanctuary. I wanted to meet those who truly loved God for Him, and not what He could give them. I continued to go to church and try to do as they did, but my heart and my spirit were bothered by what I saw and felt. It was such an insult to me. I started to volunteer at the church bookstore on Saturdays, and I was seeing what I did not want to become. For a whole year, I volunteered because I thought this was a doorway God was leading me through. God was showing me the difference between the wheat and the tare, the learned and the unlearned. He wanted me to know the what was Spirit and what was flesh.

We sit side-by-side in our churches. However, the Spirit will bear witness to the Spirit. He will show you who has God in them and who just acts like they do. "No matter what, even if you make the wrong decisions, all things work together for your good to them that love God and are called according to His purpose," *Romans 8:28*. He will lead you and He will guide into all of His truth, however, you must desire to know and use the information for ministry purposes.

Oh, my goodness! What I witnessed, and what I heard behind closed doors, was far from what was being preached from the pulpit. It was effecting me so much, I did not know who to believe. Everyone was so different after service, compared to what I knew them to be during the service. It was like night and day. One minute, people were lifting up hands and singing praises. The next minute, they would be reprimanding me for asking too many questions or dismissing me from their presence. I was not important to them at all. I guess I was a bit inquisitive, but I wanted to know, and I mean really know. People think because you are a new convert, God doesn't speak to you. I know God speaks to those who are listening.

I saw so much while attending these services, and as I was volunteering. I thought many times: "What in the world am I doing here?", but I just kept coming. It was due more to obligation than learning anything. My dad had told me to stay away from those faith-generating churches because all they wanted was my money. You know ,what he said really had some truth to it. It was only after I left this church, and was without a place to go for spiritual enrichment, that I began to see what God was showing me all along. Where you sow your seed is what will produce a harvest, if any at all. This meaning that where you sow your tithes and offerings, if the soil is unfruitful, you will never reap a harvest from it. I am sure there are many out there that can relate to this. I sowed quite a large amount of money over the three years I attended there, but never received a harvest. Now, I understand: it was not fertile ground. I was learning as I went, finding out things I needed to know for the future.

All I was contributing to was the lavish lifestyle this pastor and his wife had become accustomed to. Of course, they looked the part. But the heart of man is desperately wicked, who can know it?

I had not discovered that revelation yet, until I left that place and moved on. For the ground to be fertile soil, the pastor needs to be in the right, standing with the Lord and sowing his own tithes and offerings as well. If the pastor isn't doing this, and just living off the money people give him, then that is all it is. This is sad, but it is the truth in many of the churches today. It's all about the money. I think people just wake up one day and say: "Oh, I think I will be a pastor because it is lucrative." This explains why the people do not get delivered or come to hear His voice or to even know God. The pastor is in sin or not called by God for the position. It's just another way to make money off people who do not know the difference. The Word says: "My sheep know My voice, and the voice of a stranger they will not follow," in *John 10:27*. However, the people need to know which voice is His.

Pastors must be obedient for the church to flourish, as well as the sheep attending the church. If the shepherd is not hearing from God, how can he feed the flock week after week (unless he is just making up a message as a fill-in to what the Spirit of God wants His people to know or learn)? Serving in any ministry will open your eyes to see much more than being just a member, because you will not know what is hidden behind closed doors. But God does know. God does not want nor need members. He wants His people to know that He is God, and He will reveal Himself to each one of us!

After a few years, I asked the question about what goes on behind those closed doors. The pastor and his wife come out and always looked so groomed and polished, but I knew there was more to it. Lo and behold, God opened a door for me to begin working there. I put in my application because I was retiring from my current job after twenty years. I was interviewed four different times by four different people on staff, and I was selected out of over 200 applicants. During my employment in this church, God showed me many things, but the one thing that stood out in my mind: how to be gracious in an otherwise ungracious position.

I was in an administrative position, so I was supporting the executive pastor's wife and two other pastors who worked there. I did not know how to write a letter of correspondence at all, and many times was told to just rewrite it. It was like going back to school to learn how to read and write all over again. Iside the church, people speak a different language, meaning a matter of protocol. It was man's way of doing what they thought God wanted them to do, but all it ended up being nothing but a performance. There is no difference inside the church than there was outside the church: people just seemed to dress the part to look important. I wanted more than a new dress to wear every week. I wanted to know the God who they preached about, but no one seemed to know Him.

The first week I worked at the church, I was invited to attend my first weekly staff meeting. Honestly, I was not at all informed when it came to church business, because I thought the pastor worked at the church Monday through Friday, eight-to-five, like a secular job. To my surprise, he rarely came to the church location until our Wednesday or Sunday services. I was being taught from the ground up.

There were four new people who had recently been employed there. Towards the end of the meeting, we were all asked to stand up one at a time, and give our names and a brief description of why we wanted to work at the church. I was told to speak last, not realizing why. I introduced myself, and began to say what was really in my heart. I expressed I'd recently retired from a company after working there for twenty years and my salary had now gone from $50,000 a year to $18,000. God had so blessed me through my 401k that I was able to pay off debt, so I could live reasonably off the salary they were paying me for working there.

Well, everyone began to laugh, but I didn't quite get it yet. The pastor said: "What do you mean by that, Rebecca?" I quickly realized what I had just said, and probably turned twenty shades of red. I just sat down while people in the room began to comment: "What an ingenious way to ask for a raise after only working there one week."

Again, more laughter from everyone, but I was horrified by it. After I had gone home that evening and cried, I realized what God had just done and how He had used me to let it be known. Everyone thought I was truly unqualified to be there, but God wanted this pastor's undivided attention. The pastor and his wife were living high off the hog with all the money from church attenders giving tithes and offerings. It was enabling them to live a lifestyle of wealth with fancy cars and a beautiful home in an upscale residential area, but he was not feeding the flock: in other words, not tending to the sheep of this fold God had placed in his hands. He was a rich businessman and thought this entitled him to continue to live the way he was accustomed to. Only he must not have realized that God was watching him, and how he was not taking care of the sheep in this church. I wanted to talk about this because people have a right to know what really goes on inside the modern-day churches. It was never a God-intentioned idea for His people to be in lack, with the people running the church in plenty. God said: "All my people should be in prosperity, not just a few, but all."

What God was saying to the pastor was: "You are living above and beyond, yet your church is not properly staffed with enough people, and the ones there are poorly paid, compared to what was expected of them." This was a church with a congregation of more than 10,000. The staff was overworked and underpaid, and God wanted the pastor to know He was displeased with the unbalance in the ministry. *James 4:6*, says: "God resisteth the proud and gives grace to the humble."

I do not know how this happened, but I do know that this pastor began to minister to the church how God dealt with him about pride. God will always give us warnings first to get our attention on something we are doing wrong He is displeased with. Especially those in ministry: that is where it starts. I must honestly say, at the time I did not realize the impact that scripture had made, but I was soon to find out.

God has used me many times to tell someone what the Lord has on His mind about an individual, even if they are the pastors of their own church. It is not a salute to me, by any means. It is not easy to be sent to a church, only to find out it is in error and to have to minister the correction. Many times, they will not receive it from someone who is considered unknown, but God will send others to confirm it. Yes, and I was used many times to be the one to tell those behind the pulpit to get it together. I was also learning many ways to please the Lord along the way, and to stay away from those who refuse to obey God. It really does not matter, because it could be the CEO of a large corporation. God will only allow the wrong for a certain amount of time, and then He will allow that person to fall for all to see.

I was still working in this same ministry, and had recently received a letter from the child support division of welfare. The letter stated my daughter's father owed me $36,000 in back child support. I had filed for this many years ago, but because my ex-husband always quit his jobs to avoid paying the amount (according to the decree from the courts) I had forgotten all about it.

I went to the pastor over the prayer ministry first and asked for his advice. He said: "Rebecca, get him for all you can." So, I thought about it, and it honestly did not settle well with me. While working at my desk, I asked a second pastor for advice on what to do. "Pastor Greg", I will call him, said: "Come into my office and take a seat. I want to tell you a story." During this time, he told me a story about God's mercy. He said: "Rebecca, when God presents an opportunity to give mercy to someone for a wrong they have done to you, give them mercy."

This meaning when you give mercy, then mercy will be stored up for you when you may need it. I took the second pastor's advice, tore up the letter, and did not think about it again until now (to write this for another person who may be in a similar situation). Thank God, because when I did what I did, I was given mercy later in my walk with Him. I won't bother with the details on what I needed the mercy for, but God knew. You see, we are all tried and tested for different things in our life. It's how we respond, and the intent of how we respond, for our promotion from the Lord to come. At the same time, we are given promotion, where and how we are trained was for this moment: when God exalts us to a position He knows we have been trusted for.

Let me say, God will give us moments in our life that we are to cherish and always remember. My mother was sick on and off throughout her life. When she passed it was sad, yet liberating. I knew where my mother was, because I had been prepared for her death long before it happened. I mentioned earlier that my mother had a mental illness, and the doctors had her on all sorts of different, hard drugs. They deteriorated her organs and ultimately caused her death. My mother knew she was going to die. She sent my father to go for some wine that morning, although my mother did not drink. He went and in his absence, God took my mother home. When he returned, only after calling her name, he found my mother looped over in the bathtub. She had fallen backwards into it. Of course, my father called the paramedics, but after about an hour with her not responding, my father announced: "Let her go." So, they stopped working on my mother, and she left us.

I watched as my siblings went to pieces when our mother passed, but I had an assurance in my heart and knew where she was. It was hard to go through the next few weeks, with the funeral arrangements and the emotional things you experience when a mother or father pass unexpectedly. However, about two months after the burial, my daughter came downstairs one morning and told me she'd had a dream.

In the dream, my daughter said she was visiting with her grandma, and they were sitting on a couch in a big white room (in fact, everything was white). She said grandma was young again, like in her graduation picture from college. They talked for a while, and when it was time to leave my daughter opened the door and motioned for her grandma to come along also. My mother looked at her and shook her head and said: "I can't come with you, I must stay here."

Then she woke up. God was showing my daughter in the dream my mother was with Him, so she wouldn't fear or be concerned about her. She was fine, and we would see her again someday. Our children are innocent, so when they come to you with their dreams or what they may hear or even see, pay attention to what they tell you. There's amazing comfort in knowing this. God was clearly talking to my daughter through dreams, however, it was the most wonderful feeling to know she had crossed over safely.

I forgot to mention: forty-five days prior to my mother's death, a friend of mine went with me to visit her at a twenty-four-hour care unit, and there my mother accepted Jesus Christ to be her Lord and Savior.

CHAPTER ELEVEN

Many things have happened to me as I began to know the Word of God by experience, in other words: walking through the Word. This will take you to another place in Him, so when you hear His Word preached, you will know if the Revelation is being taught or if it is something they just made up that morning to sound good to the congregation. He said: "Feed My sheep." Then He said: "Feed My lambs." He did not say to talk with them. "This is spiritual food being released to My flock for them to survive and prosper."

When God Almighty wants you to know something, it is best to get it from the One who inspired those to write it in the first place. From Moses to the Apostles, they were all given instruction from God on how to write the Word, and what was to be said to the people of God throughout the Bible. Know His Word and His voice, and no wolf in sheep's clothing will ever be able to fool you.

I remember when I was at a church, and a person I'd become acquainted with began to mock me for something God had revealed to me. I'd made the mistake of sharing it with her. I was very upset at first, until God gave me *Matthew 7:6*. He told me: "Give <u>not</u> that which is holy unto the dogs, neither cast ye your pearls before swine, lest they trample them under their feet, and turn again and rend you." This was a very powerful moment in my walk with the Lord, because I thought this person was a Spirit-filled Christ and a friend of mine. But as He began to reveal His Word to me, by allowing me to really experience it, then I understood. It took me to another level of knowing what the Word means. You must be made aware of those who go to church, but do not have a personal relationship with God, meaning <u>No Holy Ghost</u>! If you believe in God, but not have spent any time with Him to know His voice through the Holy Spirit, you are flat missing out on what this walk with Jesus Christ is all about. You want to be connected to those who *do* have a relationship with God. If they are not hearing His voice, how can they give you good instruction or sound doctrine?

I knew then not to share those precious things the Lord revealed or had spoken to me, but to keep them to myself until the appointed time. He was protecting me from those who knew nothing about God, just acted like they did. In *I John 4:1*, He tells you: "Beloved, believe not every spirit, but try the spirits whether they be of God; because many false prophets have gone out into the world." He showed me what place I was in with Him. I needed to trust God more. I did not want to be involved with those who claimed they were Christians, when they were not. You cannot only read the Word to memorize it and sound like a Christian, you need to read the Word, allow the Holy Spirit to minister to you about His Word, and get it into your heart before The Adversary tries to steal it back. Read the Parables on the Sower found in *Matthew 13:18-23,* and you will have a revelation of what I just said. "Remember, the wheat (God's children) grow up with the tares (enemies of God) and you will know them by their fruit," *Matthew 7:18.* These are two excellent scriptures to understand those who belong to God and those who don't.

We sit in the same churches. When you encounter a tare, it doesn't always register as to who they are at first, but as you pray, God shows you. In the end, it is the angels who separate the sheep from the goats, or more commonly known the wheat from the tare. When you read *Matthew 13:37-42,* it will reveal to you what you need to know. When God shows you something in a person, it is not for you to broadcast it. It is for you to pray for that person. If God gives you anything to do or to say to them, He will make the appointed time in which to do so. Many times, it is just the prayer that changes the person, because the Holy Spirit moves on the prayers of the righteous.

I do not want to sound arrogant about what I am writing in this book. However, there were many times I did know more than what I heard from the pulpit. Why? Because I was reading it for myself! I would sit down with my Bible, and invite the Holy Spirit to minister to me His Holy Word. My relationship with God gave me spiritual knowledge, spiritual wisdom, and spiritual understanding. I took the time to do this.

It was good for me to know why I needed to know the Word of God for myself: to discern for myself and walk by faith, to hear His voice, to learn His ways, and to avoid collisions or shipwrecks (as some people call them) when we do not know God's Spirit. The Comforter will help us, and my spirit was understanding each time I heard a word contrary to what God had already taught me. I already knew because it did not bear witness inside. It's called the check of the Holy Ghost. He is just letting you know: "That's not Me" or "That is incorrect."

For those who are called into ministry, walk in a higher-level spiritually. He reveals Himself more and more for you who minister to those who want or need desired prayer. You will hear the Spirit of God telling you how to pray or what to say. Some just want to be called a Christian, like it's a club, but there are those of us who are called to know God. You will go through so much more to gain a spiritual understanding of what it is to serve the Lord, so you can serve His people. A servant learns to serve by serving the Master. It is a huge difference. God is trusting you and teaching you how to trust Him!

Some people are content with just the surface knowledge of the Word, but when God wants to take you higher you must cooperate with Him to avoid making mistakes. "My people are destroyed for a lack of knowledge," *Hosea 4:6*. I wanted to know more, and I needed to know more. God had a purpose for my life: not a walk in the park. I wish it would have been that simple, but when you have spirits coming up out of people, or demons landing on your roof at night, I can assure you there is more to the Spirit Realm than people know. The question is: can you handle it and do you want to fulfill you're God given purpose!

God means for all His children to know Him in the Word for themselves. This will enable you to define the true sheep from the wolves in sheep's clothing. Believe me, I have seen this happen and it was awful to know others could have avoided premature death or disasters had they gotten the knowledge of the Word and were established for themselves, rather than believing what they heard from the pulpit. Ask God for spiritual sight to see who is teaching the Word. It is not always a servant of God, it might be a hireling—or worse a demon. You must know the difference!

Be sure your calling is mandated from the Lord, and you have gone through the process before you just go out and start doing what you are doing without the knowledge of God's authority, as you work in His Kingdom. This explains why churches fold up or are abandoned, because people try to profit off God's people without knowing God. You can do more damage than you think to those who are innocent enough to believe what you are saying, without any truth being in it. Anyone can copy a message, repeat it, and make it sound like it came from God. It is a calling, not a job!

People want to believe what God is saying, but is it really God who is doing the talking. You must be prepared to be a preacher, teacher, evangelist, prophet, or pastor—and know what His calling on your life is. I know, because He called me by my name: "Rebecca." I really dismissed it in the beginning, because I had no understanding at that time.

Even as I began to attend church, I knew many times when the Word was being spoken out of context and out of order.

They sound good and they look good, but you must know the difference from a hireling (wolf) from a true shepherd. It is so important for all of us to know the Word for ourselves. Then we can discern between the message and the messenger. God will open your spiritual eyes to see what is invisible to everyone else. It was the knowing in my knower that God had placed in me when I was born again, not being just baptized with water: I was baptized with the fire of the Holy Ghost. This is the process for purification. I hope and I pray that as you read this book, it will begin to register some things to you. You may have already experienced some things, but did not understand why they happened or what they meant concerning you. It is time for you to pursue the Lord and find out—don't make the mistakes I made.

God is a revealer. One day He showed me *Jeremiah 33:3*: "Call unto me, and I will answer and show you great and mighty things thou knowest not." From that day forward, I began to ask God things others would not have thought to ask. I was young and innocent in spiritual matters when I started out, but as I begin to ask God the questions only He had answers for, He would tell and then show me.

You might say: "Why do you even want to know those things?" For some reason, I just did. I pursued God and He invested in me. Stay open to change because it will happen, I guarantee it. And so, I began to trust God more than man. I heard His voice, and this gave me an assurance no man had ever given to me before. He began to build my confidence, and at the same time gave me balance so the knowledge He gave me was also keeping me from any pride. Very important! I stopped watching the performance of man and started seeking the Lord, to know the Word is to hear His voice in the Word.

No, I did not always get it, but the Lord is patient with all of us who walk with Him, so His Glory can be made known. In *I Corinthians 1:26-28*: "For ye see your calling brethren, how that not many wise men after the flesh, not many mighty, not many noble, are called; but God hath chosen the foolish things of the world to confound the wise, and God hath chosen the weak things of the world to confound the things which are mighty, and base things of the world and things which are despised hath God chosen, yea, and things which are not, to bring to naught things that are." I am a Word of Knowledge person. God put it in me to know, and He also put it in me so I would have a desire to know I would teach others.

Why? Because in *Verse 29* you will read and understand" "That no flesh should glory in His Presence." In other words, they will know when the unveiling is revealed, there is no possible way you are who you are, or have accomplished the things you have accomplished, without God being involved. This is how He gets the Glory! People tend to dismiss before the time of revelation, and then suddenly those you thought would never make it are doing things only God could do in them and through them. The Lord once told me, in this order: people assess others, come to a quick conclusion, and then dismiss so quickly that they miss what God intended. Those who are called and only those who think they are called, many would never qualify for God's use or be significant to do anything. In their eyes they are already ready, but are just sadly mistaken. It took years, upward of twenty now, and I am still learning.

But when God gets ahold of you, the impossible becomes possible, the unimaginable becomes reality, and those that were kicked to the curb, ignored, or moved aside, will be acknowledged as great due to God's hand being upon them. He will prepare a table before you in the presence of your enemies in *Psalm 23:5,* and he does this to show others you are valuable. No, I could never do anything on my own, but one thing is for sure: the same blood that saved me is the blood that saved others. I just understood the power of the blood.

God is not a respecter of persons. He already knows who will respond to Him and how long it will take. So, He chooses those others dismiss on purpose, because what you discard or disregard may be rather significant to the Lord. He already knows how it will turn out: just trust Him and allow the beauty of God in your life to be displayed for others to see. Your light will shine because of the Spirit of God in you and His countenance upon you. Others seem to miss this and apply for a position God never intended for them to have.

You see, God really does not care about anyone's opinion concerning you. This is just the flesh trying to have a say, when God did not even ask. All I wanted was to be truly loved, and this was a love I was getting to know. I was despised, hated, scorned, and mocked all through my earlier life, but God said otherwise. The many times I would cry because someone rejected me, or spoke against me, or treated me unkindly and hurt me, God protected me from hearing what was said. Until you receive revelation of who you are by His Spirit, and how powerful we are using our weapons rightly that God has given us, you will not understand what can happen to you along the way. Take the time to know your spiritual weapons in *Ephesians 6:11-18* and *2 Corinthians 10:3-5*. I also found *Psalm 89:20-24* and *Psalm 91* to be something I prayed for my family and myself every day.

"This will increase you to fight the battle, the Word strengthens you to win! So, the day will come to say: I have fought a good fight, I have finished my course, I have kept the faith, and now I can enter in." *II Timothy 4:7*

On the spot, Obedience!

I had asked the Lord to use me significantly, however, I really did not know it would be in this capacity. One morning, I needed to go to my cleaners to pick up some clothing I had dropped off earlier that week. Once I pulled into the parking lot, I felt a usual feeling in my spirit. As I came closer to my location, I saw about five men outside of a DMV standing there, apparently waiting for their number to be called or possibly waiting for others to come out of the facility. When I drove by them, I realized they were looking directly at me. God had a message to be delivered today.

I pulled my car around the curve of this mini shopping mall and went into the cleaners to pick up my clothes. As I returned to my car, I heard the Holy Spirit whisper to me: "Go tell them about Jesus." Well, at first, I did not want to participate in this at all because they looked like a motorcycle club. These men were burly-looking and quite big in their stature. However, He kept repeating this statement to me three times. So, under conviction, I decided to walk over to those men. I proceeded to tell them about the Jesus I knew, but it was for them.

As I approached them and began to speak what I was sent to do, one by one I watched them all walk away from me. I was feeling quite distressed to think the Holy Spirit sent me over there, but they just did not want to hear any of this. As I turned to walk away, I felt God grab me, and I began to speak like I had never spoken before. My arm raised and I pointed my finger at one man, saying, "Something is going to happen to you and you will remember this day, how you have rejected My daughter with the message of Jesus." Then I looked at him, and he had the fear of God on his face like I had never seen before. I started to walk back to my car and as I looked to my right one of the men that was with them looked at me and just raised his arms in the air as if to surrender.

I just kept walking because I did not have a word for him, just that one man. I walked back over to my car, got in, and drove home, shocked God would use me in this manner. Be careful what you ask for when you want God to use you: He will.

These encounters would happen to me again and again. Little did I know, but God heard me as I prayed this request and He would use me outside the four walls of a church. I went home and just wept because I now realized how powerful an anointing God had given me to be a messenger such as this. One thing for sure, I could not understand why people would want to destroy what God had destined for me to do. I was as a modern-day Samuel, the prophet. Amazing, what the Lord had put inside of me and to know it was from Him in the beginning—for me to know and then to speak it!

CHAPTER TWELVE

I was fired and told to leave with the last check in my hand on a Friday mid-afternoon. After I was given the notice of departure, I looked around the corner after the administrative assistant to the VP of the church walked away from me. What I saw was astonishing. She was walking briskly down the hall, flipping her hair up as if to say "Mission Accomplished". Mind you, it what not what I wanted to see. What I was visualizing wasn't the woman, but the spirit in that woman I had never seen before. God was opening my eyes to see in the Spirit that was not known to me before. It was a spirit of witchcraft that had been operating behind closed doors the whole time, and the Lord had to show me what had been going on. This made me sad, yet I felt a righteous indignation rise on the inside. I was in training mode. However, I was still very young in the discerning department. I had much to learn. He opened my spiritual eyes to see, as He knew I could handle it. Some people can walk in the dark places, but when its inside a church, it is alarming to know what is there.

As I walked to my car, I felt like a weight comparable to ten tons of bricks lifted off my shoulders. I went home only to cry myself to sleep. I woke up the next morning, still in a daze, trying to assess what had just happened to me. No one from the church called to see if I was all right. No one came by to see me or to check on me. I was dismissed by man, but I was in the hands of God. They meant it for evil, but God meant it for good. They dismissed me like I was trash being thrown out, but God said I have plans they know not of. I don't believe God intended me to stay there very long, but the way I was asked to leave was very cruel. To my knowledge, I was blamed and criticized, as to say it was my fault for the dismissal. It made me think, I just didn't belong there. But God always has a way of revealing what goes on behind closed doors. He was bringing me out to take me through another door. I was led by His Spirit, this I know. It took a few weeks, but I began to come out of it, realizing for the first time they were not my friends at all. I was laughed at behind my back, but you see, God was watching how they treated me.

God was there to comfort me, even though I really did not want to be comforted. I just wanted to know what happened to me, and where to go from here. It was a spiritual attack designed to take me out, but it did not work. It only made me stronger and that much more determined to know my God, and why this had happened. You see, I can honestly say, I had such a naïve innocence about church and people in church I really did not have the knowledge to understand all the makings of spiritual warfare. I could just feel it!

A few weeks later, I went down my deck stairs to see why there were so many bees flying around my small backyard: a little space in the rear of my townhome. I was surprised to see a huge hive hanging under my deck where I had planted a few morning glories. This beautiful flowering plant had taken off. They are considered climbers while over the fence. Beautiful to smell and such a nice display to look at each day, however, Morning Glories are attractive to bees. I went back in the house to get my weapons: a broom and a spray can of Raid. As I descended the stairs to the area where the hive was, I was ready to do battle. I knocked down the hive and started spraying. Bees were flying everywhere. I just kept spraying until I had destroyed every one of them. This may sound cruel, but I was intent on being rid of those bees who were trying to take over my property. God was showing me warfare. When I went back upstairs to claim my victory in the destruction of the bees, I heard the Lord speak to me saying: "You have just silenced your enemies."

<u>What I did not realize: my action in the natural took care of a spiritual enemy I didn't even know about.</u> The moment I went after those bees, I was really doing warfare in the Spirit. He was showing how to win. The Lord showed me all the gossip, lies, and innuendoes that had been going on from one person to the next in a frenzy of "Did you hear what happened to Rebecca?", yet adding something each time to make it much worse than what was previously

spoken. You know the game little girl scouts play while sitting in a circle? Someone starts by whispering to the closest person and then as it was repeated. It's always so much worse by the time is gets to the last person than what was originally told.

This, my friends, is the term tale-bearing being played out. It goes on inside the body of Christ all the time. Any pastor with a spiritual awareness needs to put a stop to it immediately. From the pulpit and call it out loud, otherwise, it festers and gets worse each time it happens.

So, as I put to silence all those spiritually-tied rumors swirling around me, there was now this stillness, quietness, and peacefulness surrounding me as God gave me the victory. Believe me, I did not understand why it happened this way, I just know I was victorious in Jesus's name.

This was just the one of many encounters where God would show me: not everyone is your friend and not everyone will say good things about you. They don't bother to ask the Lord, they just listen to each other thinking, believing what they just heard was the truth about you. If you want to know something about someone, ask God! He may not give you every detail of their life, but He will say this: "Oh, Rebecca, she's my daughter."

After this, I got up and decided I would move on with my life. Even though I still felt crushed after going through such a horrendous ordeal, you must decide to get up. I had been cast off, but God was there to hold me in His arms. I went to get another job, and find one I did. I went to work for a temporary agency, and they put me to work rather quickly. I was going from one temporary job to another, sometimes within a week. I had been to five different places to work. It was later I realized God was using this to teach me how to be mobile without fear. In other words, not to be afraid of the unknown, as to where or what my next assignment would be, and assuming the role of the day as it was given. If you want to be a vessel for the Lord to use, you must be willing to go where He sends you, even as it changes day to day. I call it working for God outside the four walls of a church, which is what God wants us all to do with what He gives us. People need to see the God in us, even when we don't know they are looking right at us. When we open our mouths, they will hear the difference. We have the answer they are searching for: His name is Jesus. Introduce Him to someone today.

Our responsibility as disciples of Jesus is to get fed at church, and then to use what He gives us to minister to those who will not go to church. God is not a building, He is Spirit and moves through us to reach others who do not know Him yet. He wants to fill up His Heaven, because Hell is wide open to receive any who reject the good news and the saving grace of Jesus.

Those who are in church are unaware of the danger of *I Chronicles 16:22*: "Touch not My anointed and do My prophets no harm." It's the sad awareness of *John 16:2* that people inside the church will try and kill off those who they think are useless to God, but He will protect His chosen. We carry the Word of God in us to speak to the people of God who are waiting to hear from Heaven. It is always revealed to the prophets first, then we must speak what thus saith the Lord. It seems to be an ongoing battle, where I have found for myself. I have found it's safer outside the church, than it is inside.

CHAPTER THIRTEEN

With the beginning of the plunge of our country, as it started going into recession, I believe it hit the temporary agencies harder. Companies were finding out they did not have the money any longer to staff when employees called in sick or took sick leave any longer. They were forced to reposition within themselves: to put more work on one employee or department instead of hiring through an agency for a day or week at a time, depending on the need. So, here is where I learned when the brook dries up, it is time to move from this place. I was going to have to find a real job, with the new skills I had learned while working for the temporary agencies. As I started to look for new avenues of employment, I found the skills I had learned did not carry me very far, due to the positions I was getting were just for the day or the week. Honestly, you can't learn many new skills quickly enough other than just another way to say, "Good Morning, and the companies' name." Don't get me wrong, I loved moving around, going from this company to a different one as they were hiring for one-day assignments. But when it went dry, a lot of people were effected.

I was desiring a position that was an easy commute with a new environment to work in. One day, I happened to call a company that was hiring permanent positions for a photography gallery. It was called Thomas Mangelsen's Photography Gallery. I had never heard of it before, but as I sat in front of the man who was fielding potential employees for the gallery, he must have been seeing the holy angels assigned to me because he kept looking on either side of me. I wasn't aware of this but then again, I could not see in the Spirit like others could just yet, but I did feel their presence. This man was shown: this is the one! He gave me the interview, which would give me provision for almost another full year. God is good!

Well, I went to the interview, and it was a great fit! The lady hired me on the spot, and I started work the next day. It was located at our airport, so I could commute by bus and not have to pay for airport parking. This was exactly what I desired, because it gave me the opportunity to meet many new people each day and begin a better paying customer service position than I'd had since leaving the phone company. I was on my way to another new adventure; however, I did miss the days when going to church meant a great deal to me.

So, I started watching Christian television each morning. It really gave me a more secure feeling of God, like I had never felt before. It was like getting one-on-one with the Lord in the privacy of my home, without the hard jeers from people at church I had become accustomed to seeing. I wanted people to love me as was described in the Bible, yet had not truly discovered yet. This new position was helping me get over the shock of being fired from the church position, which I thought at the time was the worst thing that could happen to me. Let me tell you, it was not. All it did was to allow me to know what God needed Rebecca to know!

I worked for this art gallery company about six months until one day, this man came in. He was walking around, looking at the photography we sold there. He was quite beautiful to look at for a man: nice blond hair, good manners, and yet, a quiet demeanor about himself. I did not know yet he was an angel. I was strangely attracted to him but could not figure out why. I approached him and asked him if I could help. He just turned and looked at me, as if to ask a question I could not hear. He decided to purchase one of our items. As we made our way to the register, he began to tell me a story of how his wife, who he thought he could trust, was divorcing him.

He told me he was going to lose close to a million dollars. When he looked my way, it was as if he were waiting for an answer he already had. I took him by the hand to tell him not to worry because whatever he let go of, God would give it back to him double for his trouble, as the Word says. Much to my surprise, as my hand was in his, I began to soar upwards toward what I did not know yet, just moving straight up. I did not know where we were going, but I felt this peace as I transcended upwards at a rate of speed that would seem like the speed of light, it was so fast. I was not frightened by any means, I just did not know the destination. It was just another way for God to define who He was, trying to get me to understand.

Suddenly, I heard my name being called back to the place of reality, and I lost the moment. I came back into the present and even though the man was still there, he had started moving towards the door to leave, as if what he came for was now accomplished. As he left, I wanted to hug him goodbye, but he walked away before I could thank him for what he just did. He was gone so quickly, and the moment had passed. This beautiful God I was learning about sent an angel in the form of a man from Heaven to give me something I needed. What he had done for me that day was more than you can imagine. Just the experience alone was so amazing: that God could give me something He wanted me to have, and had sent me an angel for a Heavenly impartation. It was the greatest feeling in the world. When I looked over at the person who had called my name, she said to me, "Where did you go?". It was as if my body was here, but I was gone. I tried to explain, but to no avail. I just did not have the words to know what had just happened to me. I believe I was on my way to Heaven to have a brief encounter with God, because I felt such peace, as I had never felt before.

Even though it was interrupted, just the thought of going upward towards Heaven at the rate of speed I was going was something I will never forget. He wanted me to know: "I am with you, and will be with you throughout this journey."

This was just another priceless moment from a God encounter. I am giving you these moments in my life for others to believe what may have happened to them. You can ponder on them to know, God was thinking about you in that time and you did not imagine it: it was real. So many dismiss the important things that happen because they are hard to explain, but just know if you told me: I would believe it because they have happened to me.

I stayed working with this company a little longer, but before I left my employment there, I met a family who came into the gallery while waiting for a flight. The lady came in with her sister and she had the cutest little boy, strapped into a collapsible stroller. I came over to them to ask if I could be of any assistance and expressed to her how sweet her son looked, who was just wiggling in his seat. She told him to stop and said "Oh, this is my little demon." The phrase took me by surprise, because I was not expecting to hear something like that from a mother. As she walked towards the counter to pay for what she was buying, I stooped down to look at the little boy and told him he was a little angel and not a demon at all. I was so upset with the mother, I told her not to imply this saying to the little boy because what she said could become true. She dismissed me, of course, even though I knew words can speak life or death. I just wanted to allow this little boy to hear and not to believe that statement that was coming out of his mother's mouth. It was all I could do to not kick her in the shin to wake her up and become a better mother to the child God had blessed her with. I just wanted to stop a word from coming to pass.

Even though people don't realize it: "Death and life are in the power of the tongue."

Soon after this occurrence, I gave my two weeks' notice, because I was missing fellowship and I wanted to be with my brothers and sisters in Christ. Many people have been wounded in the church, but I was determined to give it another chance—to be in another place and receive the preached Word again.

I prayed to the Lord distinctively to put me in another position and show me the church where He wanted me to be, so I could have good fellowship and know more about the Word. And you know that's exactly what He did! Within a couple weeks, I had a new job, and I was introduced to yet another pastor I had not known before. The first prophet was a in a pastoral position, and they were in transition. I was going to yet another place spiritually, and I was happy to learn. They may not always like you, but even in their positions, everyone must know: it is God who chooses us, not man.

CHAPTER FOURTEEN

One day, I started to watch TV and a commercial came on with this man who was preaching like I had never heard before. In my mind, I thought: "Who in the world is this pastor, and where is his church located?" Well, to my surprise it was in my city, but a little out from where I lived. I did not care, I went to the first service I could. I was so early, I had to wait in my car for at least a half an hour before the service even started. Someone from inside noticed me as I was sitting outside, but they did not invite me to come in. I had to wait until they opened the doors. Funny, the reception you receive from those who are supposed to be Spirit-filled. The service was one like I had never attended before and had never heard the Gospel taught like this. You must understand: there is quite a difference between hearing the Word taught by someone who has the Holy Spirit versus by someone without the Holy Spirit. Yes, I knew the difference right away, but I sure wanted to find out more, so I decided to come back. By the time Sunday rolled around again, I was excited to go somewhere I thought would be better for

154 | REBECCA L PORRECO

me spiritually than where I had been. I found out some of the very people who were at my previous church now came here. This time, however, I was just determined in my mind and my heart that it didn't matter because I was coming to hear the Word, not to get involved with the church members. I would not make that mistake again, by any means necessary. You must understand: it is the Spirit of God in a person that makes them stand out.

Although I still felt estranged, even here at this new church because the gossip had already beat me there, I just wanted to know the Word of God in the way it was being preached—by a prophet of God. The previous pastor was looking like quite a showman, instead of a minister, compared to this man. I know that it sounds harsh, but I want my story to be told, so others can know this goes on in God's houses more times than not. I am sure people there are out there who know what I am talking about. I needed it, and He walked me to the right place to get through the previous disasters.

You either minister the Gospel by the Spirit or you just don't. This new pastor had an anointing on him unlike any I had ever encountered before. He was preaching the Gospel by revelation, and I was now beginning to observe and hear the Word differently from the way I had heard it before. Some of our services were so out of sorts from a regular service, it scared some people away for good. He would jump over the pews to get to someone in desperate need of a supernatural encounter or deliverance. He did not care what people thought. This was not to impress anyone: it was the way the anointing would come upon him—to get to the one it was really for in that particular service.

As he would preach what he would preach, it was with an authority that just kept drawing me to be fed more of what I was hearing as a new babe in Christ. Being fed at this level was something I needed. I had asked God for it and He heard me. The more I would come, the more I soaked in the anointing and the spiritually. I kept my distance, because people were there I had met before. They would just gossip, no matter what. When this pastor would speak the Word and it would hit my spirit, I was receiving from the Holy Ghost a deposit. It was exactly what I needed, and necessary to keep me from going on to the next place I needed to be. That's not an exaggeration: just an encounter with God taking the reins and leading me to the next level of God.

Instead of coming to this kind of service, where the Spirit of God was moving, people would still be in the flesh, but they were quickly identified and dismissed as nothing more than an interruption. This prophet had great discerning, and he would silence The Enemy from speaking out. Yes, The Enemy does try to talk, but when the person leading the service walks in their God-given authority, The Enemy is silenced rather quickly.

It really didn't matter that I again did not fit in in this place: it was where God had placed me. I needed to know how God's power worked through this man of God and this is how it was supposed to be used, not played with, as I had previously experienced. God was building a new foundation within me by being under a prophetic anointing, to enrich my understanding of the Word so I could grow stronger in the Word and in the Spirit. My spirit was starving, and I needed to eat all the spiritual food I was receiving. I began to hear God's voice more strongly, and discern what I needed to know as I grew in the things of God.

I was learning at a fast rate—more of what I needed to know in the first year I attended there than in the three-plus years I had learned at the previous church. The reason I called it a place and not a church was because it was a constant warzone for The Adversary to wreak havoc on the people who attended week after week. When your gift of discerning kicks in, it really kicks in. I was in the right place to understand what it meant and how to use it. All the gifts of the Spirit were in operation at this church, and there was no evidence of this where I fellowshipped before. Sad, but true! People of God are drawn to the Spirit of God in their pastor because they know they will be taught the Word of God to strengthen them.

This previous pastor was charismatic, almost enchanting to the people. He constantly explained to those who came what he thought we wanted or needed to hear, instead of spending time with God so he could deliver the Word to bring deliverance to the people. You know the phrase: "What is on the head will be on the body." Yes, it was a church where people were saved, but no one would grow in the Word after that. It was just not being taught from the Holy Ghost. People would become stagnant and would not grow, so we were in a cycle. After a few months or even years we would begin to wonder: "Why are we not changing?"

Now when they would go to attend other churches and hear God's Word, the way it is intended to be taught, that's when revelation would come. Every church has its issues I believe, and no church is perfect, but God is not pleased. He wants His people set free from the bondages they come in with. You can bring deliverance from the pulpit without laying hands on anyone, when you preach the Word with revelation.

I was hearing God, and learning how to discern the voice of God. I just kept coming, regardless of what anyone else thought. It was lonely, of course, desiring to have fellowship. God explained to me that people would come here, then get complacent, and not want to pursue ministry. So, God kept me at a distance. When it was time to leave, I would go to walk into ministry, as His plan for me began to unfold. So, the Lord had me write my first message titled: "Tale-bearing will not be Tolerated."

Honestly, I wrote it to appease the Lord, thinking: "Nothing will ever come of this."

However, after it was written the Lord spoke, and told me to take it to my pastor. I brought it with me to church. I wanted to leave it in my car, but God insisted I bring it with me. As I walked in, I was a little unnerved because I knew the next step would be to somehow hand it over to my pastor.

The service was ending, and this was our time to pay our tithes and offerings. We would bring them to the front of the church, where baskets were provided. I took the envelope that contained the message with me, dropped my tithe envelope in the basket provided, and looked over to see the pastor standing very close. So I walked up to him, handed it to him, and said: "Will you please read this and bless it?"

He took the envelope and departed back up the stairs to the top of the platform. I want to interject here: this was highly unusual because the pastor never came down that far during or after a service. It seemed to be a way of the Holy Spirit guiding him, so I could deliver what was in that envelope. God was teaching me to obey what He told me to do, regardless of what I thought or who the intended message was for: even if it was a pastor or prophet. It just doesn't matter, I am just the messenger.

I was not trying to impress the pastor by any means, I just wanted to obey God in releasing this information to the intended party: my pastor. God was letting him know: you need to deal with the spirit of gossip in your church, which is why the Lord titled this message: "Tale-bearing will not be Tolerated." Now, mind you, no pastor wants to be told what he needs to do, especially by someone who is virtually unknown and hasn't been thought of for any kind of ministry. But God will choose anyone He will choose to use. I did not ask for this, it was given to me. —

Remember, God chooses the foolish things of the world. I fell into this category because that's what people thought of me at the time. In other words, don't speculate who God will use He will use and who He won't. By the time it came to the evening service, I had decided not to go, but I wanted to go to kow if he'd even read the message. Well, guess what? The pastor was not happy. He told everyone in the sanctuary that night, no one—and he meant no one—was ever going to tell him what to do. I heard him, but couldn't believe it. I was crushed, but over the next few weeks, each time I went to church all the scriptures in my message would be confirmed. This told me God was dealing with him about this very controversy which was plaguing the church. Talebearing was not going to be tolerated here, and this was God telling him—not me.

No, I never got to preach the message, but I know it was from the Lord. You see, when God wants to get a message to someone it is not always the most conventional way, like making a phone call. I just happened to be the vessel used that time. God gave me an opportunity as courier for this message in that church and for this pastor. Gossip is gossip, and God hates it! It was killing the atmosphere God was trying to create. Anyone who is called into ministry by God must understand God is in charge, not the man or the woman at the helm. They are held accountable.

Funny, now that I'm reflecting on this, no one (and I mean no one!) ever came to me and asked me what was the truth, swirling around what was being so viciously repeated concerning me. So, how do you know if it's true or not if you never bother to ask the individual it's being spoken about? Would you pray to ask God what the truth was about any one individual? It's amazing how people will assume so much because they heard it through the grapevine, but never bother to authenticate it. I always want to give people the benefit of the doubt before a conclusion is determined in any matter.

There were many times God would use me, as I was in training for the ministry where He needed me the most. It's a ministry I don't think many would want to have because you are being prepared to be strong, but you need to stay unknown. So, when you are sent, whether it be for an individual in a church or in the secular arena, God is giving people a chance to repent after they receive a message by someone who He chooses to deliver it.

It is a surprise to the intended party. But nonetheless, God wants to let them know where they are in error, and to deal with it when it is getting out of hand. It's a warning first. When God chooses to make someone aware of what He wants them to know, I would never consider doing it in the first place unless He orders my steps. These are not conventional messages. It must be God's timing, God's intention, and God's revelation to the individual chosen. Only those who have a strong sense of discernment of why this is done can interpret His uses. No one will ever know who we are because it is the ultimate of surprises when we show up with a message from God for them. It's called being a vessel of honor in high places!

God will vindicate you every time! It may not be right then, but He will make it known that He chose you, and not the one they so highly thought of. I wanted so much to be a part of this ministry, but they just kept rejecting me. It even got to the point of one night that I came to the service, and it was announced that anyone who had missed going forward during a previous service should go to the pastor, who would lay hands on you and speak a word for you to hear.

Well, I went down to the front. As it was my turn, much to my surprise, he wanted to publicly embarrass me instead of minister to me. He said, as he looked at me, "You came down here, didn't you?"—and in front of all these people. God was not laughing, though. He had my back. I didn't expect this at all, but the Holy Spirit was so gracious to me that I heard Him say to the pastor: "I have work for her to do." In that moment, I felt the shift of the Holy Ghost and instead of humiliating me, he began to prophesy over me. This went on for about five minutes, and the whole congregation (at that moment) had to hear what God really thought of me. It was God's way of justifying and showing me His plans at the same time.

It was exhilarating, yet I still felt the sting of the pastors would-be rejection of me in front of all those people. They didn't know what was going on, but he did—and I most certainly did. Most importantly, God did! It turned out to be quite a prophetic Word from the Lord, just for me. I was the one He was going to use, despite what others thought. No, I did not gloat, I went back to my seat, and I cried.

After a few years of going through this, even though I had learned much from this pastor teaching the Word, I again found myself in a place of desiring more from ministry, so I decided to move on. It was quite apparent I would never be allowed to minister there. It wasn't really the kind of departure I wanted, but this is what happened. I asked the Lord to allow me to leave here, so I went to the evening service and as the altar call went forth, I made my way down to the front where the pastor was standing and stood in front of him, knowing the Holy Spirit would speak for me. He just stood there for a moment as God was telling him why I came down. As he laid his hand upon my head, I felt God's peace, releasing me to move on toward what was ahead, and not what was behind me.

Most people who are called get this amazing departure to move forward in ministry, where you are called to the front of the church and blessed publicly in your release to move on and do a greater work of God. I honestly don't believe this pastor or his wife ever cared about what happened to me from the moment I showed up even to the moment of my release. Sad, but it was true. I wanted to be like others who seemed to have his favor, but I never was. I was just tolerated there, until my purpose could be revealed. God was bringing me to new ground, and it was all right with me. Rejection hurts the spirit of a man, but many times it is interpreted the wrong way, it just means direction.

<u>Let me introduce you to Jehovah Jireh!</u>

It wasn't too long after this that God wanted me to learn another facet of Himself, I had not yet experienced. I wanted to be in a better place financially than I was at the time. I decided to apply for a re-finance of my mortgage, using the current equity to include my car payment. I also included a small amount to pay off a Visa charge card bill I had. I went to the bank and applied for this, using my current income to be approved for the loan. About a week later, I began to add everything up because I knew the extra money would be available in a few days. To my surprise, I had underestimated the amount by an amount of $8,000. Yes, I said that much. But it was God who did this, because He wanted me to know what He could do about this situation, and it was powerful.

I went right into a panic and could not believe I had miscalculated what I really needed by that much. I just sat there frozen on my couch, going through the emotionally charged: "What do I do now?" I heard the Lord say to me: "I told you what to do."

I immediately got up, went upstairs showered, got dressed, and went to the bank. During this time, the small branch where I banked were located inside the grocery store where I shopped. As I walked into the store, I felt like I was walking in slow motion, and everyone was just oblivious about what was about to happen for me. If you think for one minute that God doesn't do things for His children as you are reading, you are mistaken. He is a powerful God!

It was as if the whole store had been captured by the presence of God. I went to the bank teller and proceeded to tell her what I needed. She was on the phone and whoever they were, she said: "Let me call you right back, I must take care of this customer." After I explained to her what I was there for, she made a few calls, and walked back towards me. She asked me if I could wait an extra week for the desired amount of money I had just asked for. I was expecting the response of: "Oh, I'm sorry, we will not be able to do this." But because God had orchestrated all this, it went completely differently. When she opened her mouth to say those words: "Can you wait an extra week longer so we can redo the paperwork?"

"Of course," I heartily replied, and that was it. I had been in such distress, not even forty-five minutes earlier, and now had an assurance it was all being taken care of.

Now, you must know without any information from a new appraisal on my townhome, this information wasn't even necessary. She just took my word for it and proceeded to assist me through this dilemma. I want everyone to know, had I not listened to the voice of the Holy Spirit to move when He told me to move, I may have missed out on this amazing event. I now knew who Jehovah Jireh was, my provider. You will never know who God is until you have encounters like these to show you who He really is. It is a trust I cannot even describe. I just knew what to do because I was being led by the Spirit! The outcome amazed me so much that as I tell this story and remember the greatness of My God who has delivered me, shaped me, ministered to me, protected me, lifted me, corrected me, chastened me, heard my cries, believed in me, encouraged me, comforted me, made a way for me, opened doors for me, shut doors to go through the right door, provided for me, given me shelter, vindicated me, exonerated me, been my constant companion, and died for me, so I could have life and has continued to love and care for me along this amazing journey. I am still walking with Him even today!

There are so many more opportunities I could share about this God who I did not know, who wanted me to know Him. I am hoping that as you have read this book and begin to think back on your life, you will realize this same God who wants you to know how much He loves you. Here's the Word on it!

Isaiah 45:4-5 says: "For Jacob my servant's sake, and Israel mine elect, I have even called thee by thy name; I have surnamed thee, though thou hast not known me. I am the Lord, and there is no God beside me; I girded thee, though thou hast not known me." Everyone should be given this scripture to know that even though it takes so many years and absolute disappointments in life for us to come to God, He is making you and shaping you and delivering you all along the way. There are no mistakes in God!

An Amazing Encounter!

When my father passed in February 2015, I was sad only for a moment. I remembered how much I had loved my dad, even though I had not seen or spoken to him in over five years. My family contacted me and said: "You can go to the funeral home and be there the day before the actual funeral." They did not think it was a good idea for me to attend the following day. My daughter flew in for the funeral service and she took me to see my dad, her grandfather, for the last time. As I entered the funeral home, it was as if Heaven was there waiting on me. As I drew closer to the casket, I felt such a sense of peace with the presence of holy angels surrounding the small sanctuary, speaking their final goodbyes. I walked up to the casket. My father looked so small compared to the memory I had of him, but he had this unusual smile on his lips as if to say: "I'm happy now."

Family are funny you know, we love and then we don't love, but all in all I felt so good about the passing of my father, knowing He is with our Heavenly Father now. I just knew in my heart he was safe, and I asked God what he said when he stood before the Lord. God responded with: "He was humble."

My heart was pure about God, and I was discovering through the eyes of judgmental people that if I did not have a relationship with Him the way they did, it was not good enough. Of course, they could not see me through the eyes of a loving Father as He did and who desired me, that I am loved. That was the difference! I just needed to learn not to allow people in my life who were not for me, and it was they who missed what God was doing in me. He was preparing me as one of His chosen. I have gone through the refining of the silver for the first process, and then the second process of the fire of affliction. This has taken twenty-three years so far, and I had to stay in a place of being rejected while He was doing the work, in order for me to come out as pure gold. The fire doesn't stop, it just keeps burning hotter! You ask God to use you for a mighty work, but you first must endure the entire process.

We are all being called into the knowledge of knowing Jesus was much more than someone in the form of a man hanging on a cross at the front of a church. I came to discover the difference between a Catholic and a born-again Christian: the Catholics still have Jesus on the cross, in that vivid image of Him hanging there. However, a born-again believer has a transformation in their heart, with a renewed spirit and mind, to know that our Savior is much more than the image we might have grown up with.

When you say "Yes!" to the Lord, the real journey begins. It is so important to know the Holy Spirit as you disciple someone to know where they are in their journey. You can cause them more damage in their walk if you are trying to lead someone to the cross of Christ without the One who bore all our sins. He will reveal Himself to you, and then minister through you. Being led by the Spirit is when you understand how to minister to others so as not to hinder what He has already done in them. He prepares the heart to deposit more of Him in them. It is an amazing revelation to see someone become born again when they receive Jesus. Changing darkness to light right before your eyes. What a privilege!

Let me say this, if you ever stop long enough to be observant of someone else, do not discount them so quickly. As you have read my story, you will see how God chooses the foolish things to confound the wise and then uses the simplest one to touch and to change many. In each family, God chooses one individual who He uses to bring the knowledge of who Jesus really is. I am that chosen one!

JUST A LITTLE STORY ABOUT MY

BEAUTIFUL DAUGHTER!

My daughter is biracial, meaning her mother is Italian and German and her father is African American, French, and Indian. She is my gift from God, given to me to protect, lead, guide, and train for this life. Also, for others to see that no matter who you parents are, the one who chooses is the Lord. He will put you before kings and queens while others will have to stand there and watch. Like preparing the table before you in the presence of your enemies: *Psalm 23:5*

When my daughter was only two and a half years old, I put her in a dance studio where she learned to dance tap, jazz, acrobatics and ballet classes until she was eleven years old. During this time, she was engaged in the Cinderella pageants and won Miss Aurora, Colorado when she was five years old. She expressed to me one day that she wished she had blond hair and blue eyes because they were the ones who won the contests. Now, I took this into consideration and began to tell her how special she was already. The point I'm trying to make here is God hears the little ones requests as much as He hears our requests. She wanted to win a beauty contest, and the one who created Heaven and Earth made it possible for her to be a winner.

That is the truth, and here is the proof!

Revelation of Him in my story!

Have you ever asked God: "Who am I?" or "Where am I going?" or "Why does it feel like I have been here before?"

The Lord explained to me, when I would come to those specific moments in time as I expressed to Him, "I've been here before," or "I've seen that before," or "I've spoken to this person before," but how can this be possible? In the natural, I had not.

God said: "As you walk this journey, there are times to let you know, Rebecca, you just caught up to where I have already been with you. I have walked your life long before you, only to arrive at this place. They are put there as markers to let you know, I AM: keep walking with Me. You are on course!"

You see, we go in so many directions because we do not consult God on the decisions we are making, and take for granted He is watching over us. We never bother to ask

Him, so we wind up in places He did not intend for us to be. Yet, as He directs our steps, we find ourselves right where we should be, even though we turn a wrong turn. "Walk with Me. I may be ahead of you, but I AM leading you."

These experiences would come and repeat themselves more and more often. I could not understand why I was feeling these things, or the why in my questions. As I began to realize these are all God moments and I should to treasure them, He began saying: "Hello, I have already been here, waiting, and now you know it."

At this point, I suddenly realized: "My God, this is what I felt in those moments when I am saying to myself: 'I have been here before' or 'I know that person', or at this stop light: 'I feel I know this place'. Wherever you are, you just know that you know: 'I have been here before.'" These are those times, when He simply lets you know it's all right. You are feeling this because you just met I AM in this moment.

I pray this revelation helps everyone who reads this book and will help explain to them: God is our past, our present, and our future. He never changes, He is omnipresent, and He is omniscient! He's an all-knowing and ever-loving God who is eternal to those who want us to know Him, so He can explain our lives to us.

Revelation brings deliverance!

My next four books are titled:

"We are not Wounded Warriors; We are His Chosen Heroes." It's the story about my brother and the effects of the Vietnam war, to be told to many generations, so they understand what it does to those who serve our country as individuals, as families, and as a nation. America has sown many seeds for many years into many other nations, it is time for our harvest. It's time for America to be blessed with revelation.

"It's the Same Blood." A very courageous story of being restored, and the privilege of being used by God in a very unusual way.

"How I Pray." A book to help those who really want to make a difference in prayer.

"The Testimonies of a True Prophet." Amazing details of how God used my voice, and written accounts of what the Lord will do in your life.

God bless you all and thank you for reading *"My Journey in Knowing God"*. There is a Part Two to this story!

Made in the USA
Columbia, SC
29 May 2023

17144250R00100